"I had the opportunity (or misfortune) of seeing a video that was recently smuggled out of Jaffna and has now reached London. It exposes the most horrifying scenes of civilian casualties caused by indiscriminate aerial bombing and shelling in the North by the Sri Lankan army. After seeing those scenes, I could imagine how ordinary Tamil people would respond to the government's devolution package."

This edition published in January 1996 by
L. Samarasinghe
3 Forres Gardens
London NW11 7EX

ISBN 0 9526822 0 6

Acknowledgements

I am grateful to my eldest son **Shanika Vasantha-Rajah** whose editing contributed immensely to the final outcome of this work. Also, I wish to express my thanks to my loving wife, **Lilani**, who worked day and night to finish the typing.

I dedicate this work to my three beloved sons, **Shanika, Ishara** and **Marlon**, as a tribute to their unreserved support for my campaign for a just and lasting peace in Sri Lanka

IT IS ONLY A MATTER OF TIME BEFORE A NATION SYSTEMATICALLY MALTREATED BY ANOTHER BEGINS TO ASSERT ITS RIGHT OF INDEPENDENCE. THE TAMIL NATION IN SRI LANKA PEACEFULLY EXPRESSED ITS WISH TO SEPARATE IN THE GENERAL ELECTION OF 1977. THE SRI LANKAN GOVERNMENT DENIED THE TAMIL NATION THIS FUNDAMENTAL RIGHT AND THAT IS WHY THE TAMIL YOUTH TOOK TO ARMED STRUGGLE TO CARRY OUT THE DEMOCRATIC MANDATE GIVEN BY THEIR NATION.

CERTAIN SECTIONS IN THE SOUTH OF SRI LANKA STILL CURSE THE "DIVISION OF THE COUNTRY". THIS SENTIMENT IS BASED ON AN EMPTY PSYCHOLOGICAL ATTACHMENT TO AN ARTIFICIAL UNITARY STATE IMPOSED BY THE BRITISH. MUCH MORE COMPELLING THAN THIS HOLLOW RHETORIC IS THE DEMOCRATIC DEMAND OF AN OPPRESSED NATION TO DETERMINE ITS OWN DESTINY AND TAKE ITS PLACE ON THE WORLD STAGE ON AN EQUAL FOOTING WITH OTHER NATIONS.

PREFACE

The unresolved `Tamil Question' has for many years seemed an intractable fact of Sri Lankan political life. On both sides, nationalistic feelings now run extremely deep and the brutality unleashed has often stunned observers worldwide.

The current political leadership in the South of Sri Lanka, while acknowledging that the Tamil people have suffered appallingly over the years, imagines that their grievances can nonetheless be settled by a more `enlightened' Sinhala rule.

This book challenges that assumption and also sets the Tamil struggle within a wider international context.

As I see it, the Tamil struggle for self-determination is part of an unfinished global democratic revolution which began in the West and still rages in other parts of the world today. In particular, nations that have historically been subsumed by other nations under artificially-imposed state structures are fighting to achieve a most fundamental democratic freedom - the right to decide their own political destiny - a freedom already won by most Western nations.

In Sri Lanka, the failure of successive governments to solve the `national problem' is partly due to ideological backwardness: the inability to grasp the depth of the Tamil national struggle (and its democratic legitimacy) and the failure to relate to the Liberation Tigers of Tamil Eelam (LTTE) as its genuine leadership.

But there is another, more fundamental, cause and that is the `unitary' political system imposed on Sri Lanka by British colonialists, a system which soon after Independence provided a strong incentive for Sinhala political parties to whip up communalism among the Sinhala majority in order to secure political power.

Nevertheless, with parts of the world, notably Europe, now experimenting with new state structures there is a chance that, given mature political leadership on both sides of the conflict, imaginative solutions could be arrived at which would avoid total separation and isolationism. But this can only be achieved if the Tamil nation's right of **self-determination** *is honored and if any proposed structure is negotiated on a* **voluntary** *basis.*

Unfortunately, the Sri Lankan government's recent military operations in the heart of the Tamil homeland have demonstrated the extent to which the Sinhala political establishment is still lumbered with chauvinistic prejudices.

I am more and more given to doubt, therefore, that a truly progressive approach to the Tamil people's freedom struggle can emerge from within the present administration.

Vasantha-Rajah
London

January 1, 1996

TAMIL EXODUS
and
BEYOND

An analysis of the national conflict in Sri Lanka

Vasantha-Rajah

MYTH AND REALITY

My wife Lilani and I first visited the rebel-held Jaffna territory in June 1994 in the midst of war under the previous United National Party (UNP) administration. I was working for the BBC World Service's Sinhala Section at the time and the purpose of my visit was to prepare radio programs for the benefit of our Sinhala listeners in Sri Lanka.

Our second visit to Jaffna took place in early 1995 under the new administration of Chandrika Kumaratunga, during the ill-fated peace process. That time I went as Chairman of Sri Lanka's National Television Network.

Quite apart from the sheer adventure of visiting territory under the control of the Liberation Tigers of Tamil Eelam (LTTE) and meeting the leaders of the most advanced guerrilla movement in the world, both visits significantly contributed to my understanding of the Tamil struggle.

Wide-ranging interviews and discussions I had with hundreds of ordinary people, intellectuals, Sinhalese POWs and LTTE leaders, convinced me that most of the widely-held views about the struggle and its leadership are nothing more than elaborate myths and fabrications created by Sinhala politicians, a handful of opportunistic anti-LTTE Tamil groups living in Colombo and Sri Lanka's largely chauvinistic media.

One such myth is the view that the Tigers are a bunch of fanatics who lack the support of the Tamil masses. After personally observing in action LTTE-created police stations, law courts, banks, postal networks and social services, I realized quickly that the LTTE had built an impressive de facto government which was providing efficient administration under difficult war conditions and preventing Tamil society from falling into chaos.

Contrary to popular opinion in the South of Sri Lanka, the majority of Tamil people do not perceive the LTTE as a ruthless gang of dictators oppressing them at gun-point. Rather, most people respect them as their brave `kids' who selflessly fight the Sinhala army which continually shells and bombs their homeland.

The intimate relationship I perceived between the LTTE and the Tamil masses was recently dramatically confirmed by the mass exodus of nearly half a million Tamils who fled from the advancing Sri Lankan so-called `army of liberation' that has now invaded part of their homeland.

Not only did the LTTE succeed in handling the exodus efficiently, as any smart leadership should, they were able to provide the people with hitherto untapped fertile land and a newly-built infra-structure with health, educational and other social facilities in a rebel-held territory called `Vanni', thereby creating a virtual `new town' for an up-rooted people to begin a new life.

The move left an empty land for the Sinhala forces to occupy and it successfully subverted the government's intention of imposing a `new administration' in Jaffna under military control.

The hoisting of the `national flag' in Jaffna town, meanwhile, has been ceremoniously depicted as the re-capture of rebel territory and the military defeat of the LTTE. But closer scrutiny exposes how naive this up-beat interpretation is.

While it is true that a quarter of the Jaffna peninsula has been occupied by a massive force of Sinhala troops, many people do not realize that a substantial section of the Sri Lankan army is now bogged down in `alien' territory and surrounded by a numerically expanded guerrilla force which still controls 75% of the peninsula as well as other territories within the Northern mainland and the East.

2

Ex-Chief of the Sri Lankan Air Force, Air Vice Marshall Harry Gunathilake, has clearly understood the hollowness of the so-called 'victory' over the Tigers. Commenting in the Ravaya newspaper (17 December, 1995) he totally rebuffs the current up-beat interpretation.

"After 49 days of the military operation," he notes, "the military has not been able to capture a single LTTE fighter or any of the enormous store of weapons earlier plundered by the LTTE."

He goes on to ask, "How can we regard the capturing of a city without people a victory at all? The biggest challenge for the government is to find ways of bringing people back to this empty city, but unless the armed forces are removed people will not return."

He then warns: "allocating an enormous military force to defend a city without people cannot be done and should not be done. If the forces choose to remain there then massive counter-attacks can be expected. But should we sacrifice even more troops to defend an empty city?"

SPECTER OF DISASTER

To be sure, the national conflict in Sri Lanka has reached a crucial historical moment.

The Sri Lankan state's present military adventure against the LTTE is possibly the climax of its 12-year war to crush the Tamil people's quest for independence. The People's Alliance (PA) government certainly cannot continue its war-strategy for much longer without the specter of military, economic and political disaster hanging over its head.

I have argued in earlier articles that President Chandrika's present war-effort is a culmination of the hidden-agenda that existed within her earlier so-called `peace-effort' which collapsed on April 19, 1995.

The government's strategy then was to manipulate the peace process in order to undermine the mass base of the LTTE, marginalize them and eventually defeat them militarily so that the government could impose its own solution on the Tamil people without too much resistance. Hence I argued that the Tigers were not solely to blame for the breakdown of talks.

FAILURE TO ISOLATE LTTE

After the collapse of negotiations, the government was convinced the LTTE had become sufficiently isolated from the Tamil masses. Support from Western governments and most of the Sinhala South must have strengthened this belief.

Recent developments, however, tell a dramatically different story. As government troops first moved into the Tamil homeland on July 9, 1995, backed by aerial bombing and indiscriminate shelling, Tamil people living there and abroad began to rally around the Tiger leadership as never before.

But, ill-advised by a handful of Tamil politicians in Colombo, President Chandrika Kumaratunga remained unconvinced. Perhaps her own chauvinistic prejudices - that Tamils are not a `nation' but an `ethnic minority' living in a Sinhala-Buddhist country, and that therefore the Sinhala-dominated government in Colombo has the right to redress the `grievances' of Tamils within the unitary-state framework - compelled her to stick to her military strategy.

She went on peddling the falsehood that the LTTE are a bunch of war-thirsty fanatics secretly despised by Tamil civilians who are just longing for a massive Sinhala army to `liberate' them.

But events unfolding on the battleground clearly demonstrate the opposite - that the overwhelming majority of Tamil people regard the Liberation Tigers as their trusted leadership: within 48 hours, over half a million people moved away from the so-called `army of liberation' straight to Tiger-controlled territory.

TAMIL EXODUS

That dramatic exodus of an entire people in the face of an approaching army is, I believe, of historic significance. It will go down in history as one of the most spectacular events that ever occurred in a national struggle for independence - anytime, anywhere in the world.

It also marks a tremendous political defeat for the Chandrika administration. Indeed, the capture of Jaffna will be seen in retrospect as one of the hollowest and most meaningless `victories' in the history of warfare.

The futile ritual of hoisting the `national' flag in what is empty territory amounts merely to a cheap propaganda exercise aimed at misleading Sinhala masses in the South.

And the government's efforts to cover the embarrassment by peddling the transparently absurd explanation that the Tigers **forced** half a million civilians to move out to another part of rebel-held territory in a matter of 48 hours, is an insult to the intelligence of all Tamil people.

During the second world war, when Allied forces landed in Nazi-occupied territory, people living there were able to secretly organize `partisan' groups to support the liberating forces. That is natural if a civilian population is waiting to get rid of dictatorial rule.

5

But in Sri Lanka, all the government's efforts to initiate clandestine support-groups within rebel territory, to back their `army of liberation', have failed in spite of regular propaganda by state radio aimed at winning the hearts and minds of Tamils and discrediting the Tiger leadership.

If Tamil people secretly despise the Tigers, why has the government failed to create `sabotage groups' within rebel territory, with the help of fringe Tamil groups? How come Tamil politicians in Colombo, who regularly use state radio to encourage Tamil people in the North to dissent, failed to inspire any kind of resistance within territories that came under the advancing government's forces?

And, if the LTTE administration in the North is a ruthless regime hated by the people, then how come over 65% of the population within Jaffna and Valigamam district chose to **vacate** the areas that came under government control, and migrate to Tiger-held territories?

And why, in Canada, Britain, USA, Switzerland and France (where huge numbers of Tamil expatriates live) did anti-LTTE Tamil politicians fail to mobilize even a handful of Tamils in support of the government, while the LTTE kept on mobilizing hundreds of thousands to demonstrate against the government in major cities around the world? Perhaps the government would like to suggest these mass rallies in Toronto, Ottawa, London, Geneva, Strasbourg and New York were also mobilized at gun-point by the LTTE!

One of the pro-LTTE mass rallies held in major world cities (August 1995 in front of the UN, Geneva)

A CONCLUSIVE PROOF

Still, the most dramatic aspect of the mass exodus is not the sheer number of people who fled nor the short length of time in which the move was orchestrated. Most dramatic of all is the fact that all social institutions were effectively relocated from military-occupied territory to rebel-controlled areas. This, I believe, is a historically meaningful event because it clearly demonstrates the depth of national consciousness among the Tamil people and it conclusively falsifies the stories peddled by the Sri Lankan government about the relationship between the LTTE and the Tamil people.

As soon as the University premises were relocated from Jaffna, an appeal signed by 34 University professors, including the Vice Chancellor, was sent to the Secretary General of the United Nations (UN).

It states: "The University of Jaffna has suspended its academic activities and has temporarily shifted to Chavakachcheri and Kilinochchi from where it is carrying out its administrative functions. All economic activities including agriculture and fishing have come to a standstill as a result of this major calamity and people need assistance on a large scale to restart their lives. Shortage of cash in the banks that are functioning has aggravated the problem further. Above all, **the security of the people, even in the displaced areas, is not guaranteed due to continued aerial bombing and shelling [my emphasis].** What causes us great pain of mind is the government's unholy claim that this military operation is being carried out to liberate the Tamils from the clutches of the LTTE and that the civilian casualties during the military operations are minimal. **There is no record to show that the Tamils living in the North and East ever made a request to government to liberate them from the LTTE. The majority of the Tamils, in fact, consider the LTTE as their liberators [my emphasis]."**

8

[The full text of this letter and others sent by the Jaffna Citizen's Committee, the Northern Province Principals' Association and the Inter-Religious Union of Jaffna, are included at the end of this book]

Quite apart from the political significance of the mass migration of Tamil people from Jaffna to Vanni District, there are considerable security advantages too, from the point of view of the Tamil struggle.

The very fact that the government opted for a `Broad Front' military strategy - which amounts to `steam-rolling' through enemy territory and indiscriminately destroying lives and property - shows the utter contempt it has for ordinary Tamil people, but the government now faces a problem. While the Jaffna peninsula is vulnerable to that sort of `steam-rolling' strategy, Vanni District (largely jungle terrain) is not. Therefore, Tamil civilians who have moved to Vanni will be safe from genocidal military operations of this type in future.

The LTTE was probably aware of this and so the government's latest `Operation Sunshine', which compelled people to vacate Jaffna, could turn out to be a `blessing in disguise'.

It is worth paying attention to what Lt. General Amarjit Singh Kalkat, who directed the Indian Peace Keeping Force (IPKF) in the North between 1987 and 1990, has to say on this matter: "There is more scope in this area [Vanni] for guerrilla warfare. Why? It's jungle. Some jungles are very dense. Roads are very few. The terrain therefore is not easy for movement, mobility. You cannot take your vehicles, your transport, all over. The bulk of the fighting has to be done on foot and it has to be done at close quarters. Ultimately, it's going to have to be the man on the ground. He has to face up to themilitant eyeball to eyeball... You have to go to the jungle, hunt him out, he's waiting for you..can you do it?" [Sunday Island, December 24]

According to Kalkat, there is another advantage for the LTTE in moving to areas in Vanni: "You can reach out towards Jaffna in the North and you can hit out towards the East, to Batticaloa and so on. So strategically this is the place."

Moving to Vanni, then, not only guards against genocidal military operations, it also harbors more favorable conditions for the militants to fight the Sinhala forces.

Kalkat's observations confirm my belief that `Operation Sunshine' has strengthened the Tamil struggle and dragged the government deeper into a long, drawn-out war.

DOGMATISM

How many more Sinhala and Tamil youth need to die before the Sinhala political establishment in Colombo accepts a simple fact which world history has confirmed time and time again: that it is futile to sacrifice economic and human resources in order to militarily crush historically inevitable national struggles for independence?

How many more Sinhala and Tamil youth should die before Sinhala politicians accept the fact that the unitary state imposed on Sri Lanka by British colonialists does not tally with the social realities on the island?

How many more Tamils and Sinhalese should die before these politicians realize that Tamils are not an **ethnic minority** living in a Sinhala-Buddhist country but a **nation** with a distinctly defined homeland of its own?

How many more Tamils and Sinhalese should sacrifice their lives before these `dinosaurs' of the Sinhala political establishment realize that an amicable associative state structure, which recognizes the independence of both nations, is the only way to guarantee prosperous economies on both sides?

10

BOGUS ANXIETIES

It is interesting to see how a former Senior Civil Servant of Sri Lanka and now political analyst, Adrian Wijemanne (who refers to himself as a `Sinhala nationalist') efficiently counters some of the bogus anxieties that have for many years been cultivated by Sinhala politicians in order to justify hegemony over the Tamil nation. According to Mr. Wijemanne, such fabrications have been extremely counter-productive to the development of the Sinhala nation on the island.

Responding to the widespread fear that the Tamil nation is a predator that will gobble up Sinhala areas, he notes: "The Tamil nation has never claimed anything other than their homeland which, since 1987, has been established by law as comprising the northern and eastern provinces of the former British colony Ceylon. They are fighting to eject the Sri Lankan army from the parts of this area which it is occupying against their wishes. Not an inch of the Sinhala-occupied provinces is under attack from them. It is in the very hearths and homes of the Tamil people that war is now being waged by us against them... To believe that they are more dangerous to us than we are to them is to reverse reality completely."

And to the rhetorical question frequently posed, "Can we trust the Tamils?" he replies: "the record is that it is [ex-Prime Ministers] Mr. Bandaranayake and Mr. Dudley Senanayake who resiled from solemn written agreements that each of them signed with [Tamil leader] Mr. Chelvanayakam - not the other way round... It is undeniable... that they have better grounds for distrusting us than we have for distrusting them."

11

Then he deals with the constant play made about `one-eighth of the population [Tamils] asking for one-third of the island and two-thirds of its coastline'. He says: "We seldom mention that one-third of the island and two-thirds of its coastline have been in their possession for centuries... There is no call upon `us' to give all this to `them' because they have it already... The elementary, verifiable, physical facts on the ground are the very opposite of the dismaying notion of sacrifice that we struggle with."

SINHALA PROGRESSIVES

Putting aside such myths, it is vital that progressive forces in the South, particularly mass organizations, foresee (before it is too late) the destructive path the PA government is leading the people down.

Perhaps driving the unemployed Sinhala youth to certain death at the battle-front is regarded as a `blessing in disguise' as far as the government is concerned: an effective alternative to providing meaningful employment for them.

The Trade Union Movement in the South should not allow Sinhala politicians to drive the sons of workers and peasants to slaughter fields.

In fact, the popular interpretation of the capture of Jaffna as a `victory' is totally misleading and the up-beat characterization of `Operation Sunshine' being conjured in the South is not going to hold water for long if the government's high hopes of imposing its own solution on the Tamil people turns out to be sheer wishful thinking.

No doubt, very soon, political agitation in the South - where the promise of a swift end to the war temporarily pacified unrest - is likely to gather momentum.

Already, signs of a change of perception among some of the most politically active sections in the South are emerging and these should not be under-estimated.

Recently, over 22 Trade Unions in the Sinhala South called upon the PA government to stop the war and start negotiations `even' with the LTTE. Also, some Trade Unions raised their voices to warn Sinhala politicians not to send the sons of workers to slaughter fields.

One popular weekly Sinhala newspaper called `Hiru' has just published a statement calling upon progressive forces in the Sinhala South to condemn the government's war **totally** and **unconditionally**. It asks those progressive forces (particularly Sinhalese living in the East) to withdraw their support from government forces and support the Tamil struggle instead.

It calls upon Sinhala progressives to come to an alliance with the Tamil struggle. And, condemning the government's war as a racist war, it praises the LTTE administration in the North for carrying out `progressive' reforms and making revolutionary changes to Tamil society. The paper also praises the LTTE for banning the caste system and helping Tamil women liberate themselves from male oppression and achieve equal status with men.

A BREAK-THROUGH

A newspaper-statement like this in the Sinhala South marks a significant break-through in the `Sinhala-consciousness'. Until now, none of the so-called Sinhala progressive elements (including left-wing parties) could relate themselves to the LTTE. While abstractly paying lip service to `Tamil grievances', they could never relate to the actual Tamil struggle as it was being waged on the ground, because of their prejudices against the LTTE.

A satirical cartoon published in 'Hiru' mocking the naivety of the Sinhala masses in the South being misled by the war euphoria

14

The `Hiru' statement shows it has definitively overcome that ideological gap. It clearly indicates that an important section within the Sinhala South has undergone a transformation in its perception of the Tamil struggle. I predict that in the coming period a gathering momentum against the war and in support of the Tamil struggle is likely to develop in the Sinhala South. Spiralling war expenses will no doubt hasten this process.

Already, one Sinhalese political activist in Colombo has told me over the telephone that if progressive forces in the South are committed to defeating the government's present war-strategy, which is inflicting enormous suffering on Tamil and Sinhala oppressed people alike, a clear and unambiguous stand must be taken in relation to the Tamil struggle led by the LTTE.

"A `Revolutionary Defeatist' position - openly calling for the defeat of government forces and victory to the Liberation Tigers of Tamil Eelam - would be an effective step towards challenging the government's strategy," he told me.

According to this activist, a campaign within the Trade Union Movement to call a general strike to force the government to withdraw all Sinhala forces from the Tamil homeland would also be timely. He added: "Left-wing parties which are reluctant to take such a principled position should rightly be condemned as victims of Sinhala chauvinism."

ECONOMIC NIGHTMARE

At the time of writing, the cost of the war is substantially more than the entire expenditure on health and education put together. The PA government has had to scrap the free mid-day meal for school children in the South and war costs estimated for 1996 in the government's latest budget come to 38.5 billion rupees. That is an increase of almost 19% on this year (1995).

The President of Sri Lanka recently said the government will need an additional 500 billion rupees to crush the LTTE; also that it will have to increase troops by a further one hundred thousand.

And who is going to bear the brunt of all this? Mainly the poor masses in the South of course. 65% of the population of Sri Lanka now live in absolute poverty and youth unemployment stands at 1.2 million, out of which 25, 000 are graduates.

The gaping budget deficit is an early warning signal of the unfolding nightmare. The government continues to raise massive short-term loans from the private sector to finance the deficit, forcing interest rates to rise frantically. Quite apart from the effect this will have on investments and economic growth, it is putting enormous pressure on the government to implement drastic cuts in public expenditure.

In the hope of bridging the budget deficit (at least partially) the government managed to convince the Shell company to buy the Gas assets in Sri Lanka. The LTTE has given its reply to this by blowing up the massive oil-depots in Kolonnawa and Orugodawatta.

The blowing up of oil-depots clearly shows that the LTTE is now turning towards economic targets as well. This new turn is bound to alienate the business community and foreign investors further from the government's war strategy.

Moreover, all indications are that labor unrest is set to grow. Already, the Council of the Federation of Chambers of Commerce and Industry of Sri Lanka (similar to the CBI in Britain) has urged the government to act quickly to stop labor unrest. Certain members warned that the issue was fast becoming a national problem threatening the future of **every** industry and business.

POLITICAL NIGHTMARE

This war, if it continues, will feed the conditions for deep social unrest in the South because the poor masses simply cannot carry the burden of war on the basis of chauvinistic sentiments alone.

All indications are that the government will be compelled to axe public expenditure on an unprecedented scale in the near future causing acute polarization between poor and rich. It is true that in a country like Sri Lanka, where the business community is mainly dependent on foreign markets and foreign investment, the poor masses are to an extent economically dispensable. But I do not need to remind people about the serious political repercussions of allowing the living conditions of the poor majority to worsen.

The Sinhala South has already seen two major youth uprisings - in 1971 and 1989 - which seriously disrupted the socio-political life of the country. Fortunately for the Sri Lankan state this youth movement had a monumental incapability to relate to the Tamil struggle in the North due to chauvinistic limitations.

Importantly, though, a section of the same political party which led those uprisings - the People's Liberation Front (or JVP) - now controls the Sinhala newspaper `Hiru' which has taken a clear stand against the war and in support of Tamils' right to self-determination. However, because the JVP leadership remains chauvinistic in its outlook, it has come into sharp conflict with the editorial board of the Hiru newspaper.

JVP'S CONSPIRACY-THEORY

The JVP is known for some time to have been peddling a `conspiracy-theory' laden with `Marxist' phrases to cover its chauvinistic opposition to the Tamil struggle. According to this theory the Tamil struggle is part and parcel of US imperialism's sinister strategy to break up the country. In other words, they think the Tiger leadership is being used by the American government to split the country.

This theory would be extremely amusing to the US State Department if it ever came to know about it. What became crystal clear to me in my recent efforts to convince the US State Department to put pressure on the Sri Lankan government to stop its genocidal military adventure, is that the US government is in no mood to disturb the Chandrika administration's efforts to militarily crush the LTTE.

After lengthy discussions with State Department officials, the impression I got was that they see liberation struggles of this sort (within economically-friendly countries) as mainly disruptive forces which should be crushed **if possible**. The US government would be delighted if it could persuade the LTTE to agree to a compromise-settlement within a unitary state and enable the Sinhala-dominated government in Colombo to maintain its hegemony over the Tamil people. I think it was the LTTE's refusal to betray its fundamental principles that led both the US and Indian governments to turn a blind eye to the Colombo government's ruthless invasion to crush them.

Moreover, I am convinced that the commonly-held dogma about the LTTE having a fanatical craving to split the country also falls short of the truth. What the LTTE firmly insists upon is the Tamils' right of self-determination, and this does not **necessarily** mean a total break-up. Indeed, whether the conflict ends up in partition or not will depend mainly on the degree of rigidity shown by the Sinhala-dominated government. According to Tiger leaders, the principle of self-determination is **not** negotiable; but a different, mutually beneficial state form **is**.

18

This point is clearly expressed by the LTTE ideologue Dr. Anton Balasingham in his reply to A.S. Paneerselvan, Chief of Bureau in Madras of the Delhi-based journal `Outlook'. To the question: Do you think you can win **independence** (my emphasis) on military terms? Dr. Balasingham replies: "`Independence' is the wrong word. It is our right to decide our political destiny. That is the meaning of right of self-determination."

The `Hiru' newspaper's present unambiguous stance in relation to the Tamil struggle is very encouraging and there is evidence of similar trends emerging among other left-wing groups too. But it remains to be seen whether these other groups can relate to the Tamil struggle in its **concrete** form, i.e., as it is being waged by the LTTE. Mere lip-service to the principle of self-determination is viewed with suspicion by the majority of Tamil people who consider the LTTE as their leadership. The Tamil people will continue to regard such support as abstract until a clear stand is taken in support of the LTTE.

Many signals now indicate the real possibility of a new political movement being born in the South, free of any chauvinistic hangovers. Such a movement would present a real crisis for the government.

One can just imagine the scale of the problem the Colombo administration would face if there were another uprising in the Sinhala South - this time, unlike previously, led by a party having comradely links with the LTTE and, above all, at a time when most of the government's troops are bogged down within the Tamil homeland in the midst of a hostile population and a formidable guerrilla force.

MILITARY NIGHTMARE

The PA government, which mainly represents the interests of the business community in the South, has been giving high hopes to them that the LTTE could be crushed quickly through a `high-tech' war.

But the mass exodus of Tamil people, leaving a `ghost town' for the troops, must have raised serious doubts as to the plausibility of the government's plan to install a new administration in the North. For, more than anything else, that dramatic episode has signalled the beginning of an anti-climax for the government's strategy.

The Sea-Tigers will, in all probability, continue to blow up ships and planes (paralysing supply links to troops in the North) and will go on attacking oil supplies as they recently did in Batticaloa where they blew up an oil-cargo train.

Meanwhile, making use of the breathing space found in the East, the LTTE will continue taking the area under its control while carrying out further attacks on economic targets in the South, effectively undermining the government's economic base. This would go on while over 50, 000 soldiers are bogged down in the Tamil homeland increasingly becoming `sitting ducks' for LTTE attacks.

Sri Lankan military strategists seem extremely naive to boast about killing over a thousand rebels when the advancing Sinhala army (which has so far displaced over 65% of the Tamil population) has driven thousands more Tamil youth to join the ranks of the LTTE.

Government troops are likely to end up over-stretched, over-tired, rather disappointed and surrounded by a numerically expanded and highly motivated army of LTTE fighters backed by an ever more determined people who are becoming increasingly hostile to the Sinhala government and its forces.

Now, one should not under-estimate the possibility of the most sinister forces of repression reappearing within this context. Let us not forget that the power of the Executive Presidency remains intact and if the fragile PA Alliance shows any serious signs of cracking, and if unrest in the South accelerates, it is all too possible that parliament would be suspended and that a free hand would be given to the military to crush any dissent.

Given the present climate, it may become a tempting option for the government to capitalise on the military's dazzling popularity in order to suspend parliamentary democracy and install some form of military rule to try and crush dissent in the South.

In such a scenario, the radical youth of the country, left-wing politicians, trade-unionists and also pacifists, human-rights activists and NGOs, would find themselves in grave danger. Indeed, the recent attack on a meeting of NGOs and peace activists at Bentota (near Colombo) by a gang of Sinhala extremists (with the blessings of some sections of the government) should be regarded as a sign of things to come.

INTERNATIONAL IMAGE

Developments like these, however, are bound to jeopardize the Sri Lankan government's image abroad. In fact, this is already happening to some extent. The cleverly won international sympathy for the government's `cause' in the aftermath of the failed peace process has begun to erode especially in the light of events like the government's hostile response to the UN Secretary General's plea to help Tamil refugees, the sacking of the government administrator in Jaffna alleging he had exaggerated the plight of the refugees, and the arrests of two Catholic priests taking money and goods to refugees in the North.

As such events become more frequent and as the true scale of the destruction caused in the North through indiscriminate bombing and shelling comes to light, the international community will almost certainly become alienated from the government's strategy.

In a fascinating Guardian/ Channel 4 television investigation across three continents, some journalists have exposed the trail of lies, cover-ups and carnage that were the reality behind the `clean' war in the Gulf in 1991. Writing a curtain-raiser for this TV program, Maggie O'Kane writes in the Guardian Weekend (December 16): "This is a tale of how to tell lies and win wars and how we, the media, were harnessed like beach donkeys and led through the sand to see what the British and US military wanted us to see in this nice clean war."

The way the Sri Lankan government manipulated the foreign and local media during its so-called `war for peace' was, I allege, far worse. The government openly banned foreign and local journalists from reaching the war-zone and imposed strict censorship on local coverage of the war.

Also, just as the Kuwaiti government hired a Western Public Relations firm to paint to outsiders a demonic image of Iraqi troops during the Gulf War, so the Sri Lankan government hired a similar firm to `handle' media coverage of the war internationally and to paint a demonic image of the LTTE leadership abroad.

While this is a most disturbing development in the conduct of modern warfare, in both cases the strategy has proved remarkably successful. In the case of the Gulf war it took four years for the truth to emerge. In Sri Lanka, however, lies and distortions are already being exposed.

Formerly, there existed a widespread image of the war as a sincere effort by the government to liberate Tamil people from the clutches of a bunch of terrorist thugs. But this image is starting to crack.

Eye-witness reports reaching Colombo have now revealed the ruthlessly indiscriminate nature of bombing and shelling carried out by government forces during `Operation Sunshine'.

`BROAD FRONT' STRATEGY

An analysis by Lt. General Amarjit Singh Kalkat of the former Indian Peace Keeping Force (IPKF) illuminates the utter ruthlessness of the strategy adopted by the Sri Lankan armed forces in their effort to capture Jaffna. He says:

"[The Sri Lankan military] followed a strategy of a **Broad Front**... Now a Broad Front advance is a very secure method of doing it because you can never be off-balance. But to do a Broad Front you need large forces, which they have got. It is much more time consuming. You need time, which they have got; they're in no hurry. And thirdly, it causes a lot of destruction because you are actually steam-rolling through the area. Step by step. Do a certain distance first, then clean up, converge on the next one. Any building from which resistance comes or where there is likely to be resistance, bring it down with air bombing or with tank fire... **You clean up**. But then as you pass you're leaving behind rubble as you go. So that was the other problem - for which they have resorted to censorship so that this doesn't come out... They have concentrated overwhelming force for a Broad Front and they have made sure that there is no adverse publicity. World opinion, the press, don't know what is happening there because it's all controlled." [Sunday Island, December 24]

No journalists, local or foreign, were allowed to go to the war-zone and so became totally dependent on press briefings from military spokespersons in Colombo. These briefings were often deliberately misleading. The Sri Lankan Sunday Times' editorial comment of December 17, makes the following startling and revealing attack on the government's policy with regard to censorship on military information in the press:

"Our Situation Report has for several weeks been trying to give the correct casualty figures but the censors have been diluting and doctoring the statistics. That is why our Situation Report is not giving the censored casualty figures **which are wrong** [my emphasis]. Our Situation Report of today has been slashed by the Censor. Now this is being done because the government believes such news will benefit the LTTE. But the same news could have been announced over a foreign radio or TV station yesterday even before the Sunday Times hit the streets today... So this is not only a crazy censorship, but one that seems to have a hidden agenda in not keeping Sri Lankans living in Sri Lanka up-to-date with what's happening in their own country... This and other factors go to show that the **censorship is largely a cover-up** [my emphasis]."

The government must have been well aware of the implications of adopting a Broad Front strategy in densely populated areas (a strategy which even the IPKF was reluctant to adopt). Perhaps more than anything else this reveals the shameful disregard it has for ordinary Tamil people.

This disregard was re-affirmed in the aftermath of the capture of Jaffna. A correspondent for TIME magazine, Anthony Spaeth, attended the recent ceremony held at the Presidential Secretariat in Colombo soon after the hoisting of the `national' flag in Jaffna. Describing the proceedings, his observations clearly expose the hypocrisy and chauvinistic nature of Sri Lanka's Sinhala-dominated government:

"Sri Lanka's leader stood gravely before a line of tough-looking military officers. Deputy Defence Minister Anurudha Ratwatte, fresh from hoisting the flag in Jaffna town, presented her with a scroll rolled up inside a red velvet container. The scroll was dated `full moon day of the month of Unduwap in the year 2939 in the Buddhist Era.' It read, `Your Excellency's rule and authority has been firmly re-established' in the historic city. The territory was not referred to as Jaffna, its official name, but `Yapa Patuna', the term used by [Sinhala] conquerors in Medieval times... To outsiders, the ritual might have seemed arcane and meaningless, but to Sinhalese, who make up three-quarters of Sri Lanka's 18 million population, it was freighted with implications. Kumaratunga's use of Sinhalese-Buddhist iconography carried a message: she had conquered Tamil lands and defeated her enemies in much the same manner as Sinhalese kings of centuries gone by."

A WARNING ABOUT THE PACKAGE

It should be remembered that the Sri Lankan government's much-trumpeted `political package' to pacify the Tamil struggle for self-determination came at a time when the army, navy and air force were launching their biggest ever military operation in the North and East inflicting enormous suffering on the Tamil people.

It is ironic that during the peace process the LTTE alleged the government had a hidden military intention and Jaffna newspapers carried cartoons depicting President Chandrika riding an armored car holding a dove of peace in one hand and a missile in the other. That perception has now been proved justified.

The handful of Tamil parliamentarians working hand in glove with the Colombo government have enthusiastically welcomed the `package'. But this is tremendously counter-productive.

25

For, this package seems to be part of the government's strategy to crush the Tamil struggle by creating confusion and division within the Tamil community and so the Colombo-based Tamil parties have played straight into the government's hands.

Already, the government is taking steps to dilute the devolution package substantially. The Island newspaper in its front-page leader (17 December) reports that: "An amendment has been introduced to the Devolution Package of the Government to empower the President of the Republic of Sri Lanka to dissolve any regional unit proposed in the Package, at his or her discretion".

Moreover, the government's recent act of dissolving two UNP-run provincial administrations has reinforced Tamil people's suspicions about the `new' devolution package as well. For, as some constitutional experts have pointed out, the proposed regional units do not go beyond the Indo-Lanka Peace Accord of 1987 upon which the existing provincial units are founded. (On issues such as the North-East merger, granted in the Indo-Lanka Accord, the new package is even less generous).

Perhaps by this blatantly high-handed action of dissolving the UNP-held provincial administrations, the government wanted to demonstrate to the Sinhala majority that the Centre is very much in control, thereby alleviating any remaining fears about Tamils ever gaining autonomy.

The leader of the Opposition, Mr. Ranil Wickramasinghe, has already complained that the manner in which the government dissolved the administrations "has made a mockery of devolution."

Now, in the run-up to fresh polls to be held in those two (North-Central and Sabaragamuwa) provinces in March, the government will, in all probability, try to cash-in on the war euphoria generated in the aftermath of the `fall of Jaffna'. It will try to reinforce the countless assurances already given to the Sinhala majority that the new package does not in any way undermine the Sinhala-dominated central government's supremacy.

By the time the package becomes law - if that happens at all - I suspect that any remaining pretence of it being a `federal' solution will have all but vanished.

So, as the LTTE correctly judged, the government is using this package as a mask to try and hood-wink the Tamil masses so that the Tamil liberation struggle and its leadership can be crushed.

Therefore, the Tamil parliamentarians in Colombo should withdraw their support for the package and tell the government in no uncertain terms that if it is serious about any sort of political solution it should unconditionally call off the war offensive, withdraw its forces and try to restore peace negotiations **with the LTTE**.

The reason is simple: the people of the North see the LTTE as the vanguard of their struggle for national liberation, and also need them **for their own protection**.

I myself have grave reservations about the package. As it stands, I do not think it goes anywhere near challenging Sinhala hegemony over the Tamil nation. For, any de-centralization achieved by a 2/3 majority in the Sinhala-dominated parliament can also be re-centralized by a 2/3 majority.

Also, when the package allows for central government to retain the power to abolish regional administrations under `emergency conditions', it is worth remembering that Sri Lanka has mostly been under emergency rule for the past two decades!

27

Now that an amendment has been introduced to empower the President to dissolve any regional unit at her discretion, the non-federalist nature of the proposals is becoming ever more explicit.

And, on the issue of the merger of North and East, it must be obvious to any clear-thinking person that the government is not about to budge. It is naive for Colombo Tamil politicians to hope that a government which is getting increasingly cornered by the Sinhala electorate will end up compromising on this issue.

Lt. Gen. Kalkat elaborates on this point in the afore-mentioned interview: "...the Weli Oya Kent Farm, the large area which was colonized by the Sinhalese over the last fifteen years (if you recall, the Israelis are helping them and they are trying agriculture and so on)...now that area was originally Tamil lands. It will be very difficult for Chandrika Kumaratunga to tell her party and government and the army that these people have to go!... Whether she will be able to convince them that it will become part of a Tamil province under a Tamil government, is a moot point."

From the beginning, the Liberation Tigers condemned the `package' in no uncertain terms saying it was a cover to launch the government's military offensive. More and more, it seems they were right. The government, for its part, openly announced that this was the package it was going to impose on the Tamil people and that in order to do so the Tigers would have to be defeated.

But then, within days of capturing Jaffna, the government has already begun the process of diluting the package.

It is not difficult to see that the PA government has become easy prey to the `majority-rule syndrome' inherent in the unitary-state system imposed by the British colonialists. And the government's present over-riding objective seems to be finding ways of cashing-in on the euphoria generated among the Sinhala majority through false propaganda about `defeating the Tigers'. But as Lt. Gen. Kalkat has admitted: "The fall of Jaffna does not have a military significance. Neither does it have a significance in the military aspect of the LTTE operations."

I would go even further and say that the government's military adventure has **strengthened** the Tamil struggle. Not only has it helped to numerically increase the LTTE's fighting force, it has also hardened Tamil people's resolve to fight for a separate state.

The government, however, does not seem to be much concerned about such implications. Presently, its biggest interest is to somehow make use of the `victory euphoria' among the Sinhalese to achieve political gains, in a snap general election if possible, before that euphoria fades out.

Therefore, the efforts of Tamil politicians in Colombo to convince the President of the importance of improving on the package will amount to a sheer wastage of time and energy. The over-riding momentum at present is to dilute the package, not improve on it.

MACHIAVELLIAN TACTIC

It seems the Colombo Tamil parties have become roped into the government's Machiavellian tactic to install a `new administration' under military occupation. Therefore, their requests for a cease-fire on both sides without at the same time demanding government troop-withdrawal will amount to a treacherous collaboration aimed at overcoming the government's present dilemma of having control over an **empty** area of land.

A cease-fire would be used as a sinister cover to bring the Tamil parliamentarians to Jaffna safely so that they can appeal for people to return. Already the government is distributing leaflets from the air offering lucrative financial incentives to Tamil civilians who comply.

The Tamil parliamentarians in Colombo should realize that the proposed `new administration' is a cover to smash the Tamil liberation struggle and maintain the Sinhala-dominated government's hegemony over the Tamil nation.

It is encouraging to see that at least one prominent Tamil politician in Colombo, Kumar Ponnambalam, has understood and spoken out about the reality behind the government's military adventure. I quote from his article which appeared in the Sunday Leader of 24 December:

"Of course, it can be easily said that the LTTE is preventing the Tamils from returning [to Jaffna] but has not history taught us, replete with instances, that even the gun cannot stop a mass uprising? If the Tamils are not with the LTTE is this not the most opportune time to break all shackles, defy the LTTE and as a mass movement start towards Jaffna, specially when there is a President waiting with a dove in hand and a Sinhala army waiting at hand to give succor? Let us wait and see."

Speaking about the euphoria after the capture of Jaffna, he cautions: "If this is the reaction of the Sinhala Nation for the capture of a ghost town, with the full might of the LTTE unassailed, let the Tamils be warned what would happen if the LTTE is removed from the center-stage. It also shows the utter hatred a preponderant section of the Sinhala people have towards the Tamils. The hatred is pervading the air and permeating into every nook and corner. Is it not obvious, even to the most die-hard Sinhalese, that the only answer or alternative to all this must be a separate state?"

Then he makes a thundering attack on the Tamil politicians who are collaborating with the government and challenges the feasibility of implementing a new administration with them in Jaffna: "At least now, let the President know that she cannot go anywhere with the discredited Tamil quislings and cohorts who surround her in Colombo. They are, at most, plain sycophants who only live on her and who cannot even get out of their buildings in Colombo alone, much less be of any assistance to her or the government in the North or East."

Such comments could foreshadow a potentially serious crisis among the Tamil political establishment in Colombo.

But as for the government, if it really means to implement a lasting solution it must immediately halt its military offensive, withdraw its forces and stop issuing ultimatums to the LTTE in a provocative manner.

Further, if the government is serious about achieving a viable solution it should come up with an honorable way of implementing the final agreement. Relying on the Sinhala community's verdict to determine the Tamil nation's democratic right of self-determination seems to me absurd and unacceptable. National democratic rights are non-negotiable. What is negotiable is the **form** a future confederational state of Sri Lanka and Eelam might take. The present terminology of the Sinhala government - using words like `devolution' and `concessions' - also seems inappropriate and insulting.

MILITARY OFFENSIVE

But let us not forget what is going on in the North and East right now. Over 50, 000 Sinhala troops have entered the Tamil homeland backed by air and naval forces, displacing over half a million people and causing many civilian casualties. The final offensive on Jaffna, code-named `Operation sunshine', was the climax of a series of operations.

The first, `Operation Leap Forward', began at dawn on the 9th of July. The military warned civilians to clear the areas Southwest of its base at Palaly, recommending churches and temples as shelters. But the horrific events that followed are told in an article that appeared in TIME magazine on the 31st of July:

"At 4.30 pm, an Argentine-made `Pucara fighter' flew toward the Navali church, 3 kilometers outside the combat zone, and bombed the sanctuary and an adjacent courtyard. Most of the people huddled inside were women and children, many of whom were killed immediately. Others had limbs blown off. Survivors were brought by tractor to the town of Jaffna, 6 kilometers away; but, the Jaffna Teaching Hospital and its lone surgeon weren't prepared. They soon ran out of bandages, antibiotics and beds. `The treatment was crude,' said the Protestant Bishop of Jaffna, who rushed to hospital to help. According to him, `limbs that could have been saved had to be amputated.' The military denies bombing the church, but residents and the International Committee of the Red Cross confirm the bomb attack."

Meanwhile, corpses of young Tamil men, many with faces mutilated to prevent identification, have started showing up in lakes and fields outside Colombo.

Tamil civilians bombed in a church after being instructed by the Sri Lankan military to take refuge there

Innocent child victims of Sri Lankan air force's church bombing

Government tank being blown up by LTTE forces during the
Sri Lankan military's 'Operation Leap Forward'

Sri Lankan air force's Puccara aircraft being shot down by LTTE forces during the government's 'Operation Leap Forward'

The Sea Tigers in action

The `Killing Squads' with military connections who thrived during the UNP regime, have surfaced again under the new government this time to kidnap and murder at random Tamil youth living in the South, just as these same killing squads prowling in white vans without number plates used to terrorize Sinhalese youth killing over 60, 000 youngsters between 1988-1990.

`Operation Leap Forward' was presented to the public as **part** of the military's strategy to capture Jaffna. It was described by the Colombo Press as an attempt to `liberate' the Tamil people from the `clutches' of the Tamil Tigers.

The initially captured areas around the Palaly army camp were portrayed in the Sri Lankan Press as `liberated land' which would be used as a `springboard' to launch the more decisive stage of the offensive to `free' Jaffna.

Right from the beginning, the government tried hard to present its efforts to capture Jaffna as qualitatively different from previous ones. For, this time, the government seriously believed it had successfully convinced the Tamil masses that the `war-thirsty' Tamil Tigers were solely to blame for the collapse of peace talks and that, therefore, the peace-loving majority in the North (who, in the government's naive view, secretly despise the Tigers) would welcome the Sinhala troops with open arms.

ARMY OF OCCUPATION

They got it wrong. The Sinhala army presently roaming in the North is seen as an army of **occupation**. And quite rightly so, that is exactly what they are.

Radio programs from state radio in Colombo targeting listeners in the North have been bombarding Tamils with appeals to rise in support of the Sinhala army. Some time back, the Minister for Housing, Construction and Public Utility, Mr Nimal Siripala de Silva, made a special trip to the North to promise generous hand-outs to the Tamils in so-called `liberated' areas presumably in the naive hope of bribing Tamil people to change loyalties.

However, none of these tactics have worked as expected. On the contrary, able-bodied men in and around captured areas left their villages in droves to join the rebels as soon as troops entered.

Now that the military effort to `save the Tamil people' has gone contrary to expectations in the face of a mass exodus of Tamil people, one of the basic notions underlying the government's strategy comes into question, i.e., the notion that once the government could demonstrate to Tamil people in the North that it could install an alternative administration backed by a heavily-armed military force, Tamils would drop the LTTE like a `hot potato'.

HIDDEN AGENDA

This assumption dominated the government's earlier peace-effort and, subsequently, that effort became nothing more than a `tactical episode' to crush the Tigers. Instead of trying to cultivate **trust** with the Tiger leadership the government attempted to drive a wedge between the LTTE and the Tamil masses.

This explains the apparently schizophrenic behavior of the government during negotiations. Many people thought it was due to lack of professionalism but in fact it was due to a **hidden agenda,** which was to isolate the Tigers in preparation to crush them militarily.

So who can blame the LTTE for pulling out from the peace process? Why should they willingly walk into a `mouse-trap'? In all probability, the LTTE's own intelligence sources must have prompted them to pull out of talks even at the risk of jeopardizing their image internationally. They took the gamble and alienated the international community quite substantially as a result.

So the present military offensive is the culmination of a well-calculated strategy originating from the peace process itself. It is also the `acid test' of the theory advocated by the government think-tank and the military establishment that the LTTE could be marginalized.

But every indication so far confirms that the Tamil people are not about to betray their leaders.

LTTE AND TAMIL STRUGGLE

Just as F.W. de Klirk did not try to drive a wedge between Black people and the ANC and just as the Israeli government realized that there was no way it could drive a wedge between the Palestinian people and the PLO, the Sri Lankan government too should learn quickly that they are making a costly mistake in trying to isolate the LTTE from the Tamil masses.

Just as F.W. de Klirk and the White regime in South Africa understood that they had to undergo an ideological transformation which many observers thought impossible - i.e., rejecting apartheid and introducing a `one-man-one-vote' system - and just as the Israeli government had to undergo a similar ideological metamorphosis - in accepting the concept of Palestinian self-rule which would eventually lead to a Palestinian state - in the same way, the Sri Lankan government will have to get used to thinking of the Tamil people as a separate nation with a right to self-determination.

It has already become clear that the Chandrika leadership has not grasped the historical content of the Tamil liberation struggle any better than its predecessors. It has not grasped that Sri Lanka has historically evolved as a society consisting of two main nations, Sinhalese and Tamil, and that although the Tamil nation is numerically smaller in relation to the Sinhala nation it has evolved side by side with it, retaining a distinct identity while closely interacting with it. And a clearly identifiable `Tamil homeland' has emerged over a long historical period.

Indeed, as Adrian Wijemanne has recognised: "The Sinhala people are a nation possessing, like all other nations in the world, a language, a literature, a culture, a morality and a territory which they physically occupy - the seven predominantly Sinhala-occupied provinces on the island - and to which they are rooted... I believe the indigenous Tamil people on the island to be, also, a nation possessing every one of the attributes mentioned above, the territory predominantly occupied by them being the northern and eastern provinces on the island... I do **not** believe that a Sri Lankan nation exists for there is no Sri Lankan race, no Sri Lankan language, no Sri Lankan literature, and no Sri Lankan morality. The Sri Lankan `nation' is a myth concocted with the deliberate intention of giving legitimacy to a Sri Lankan state comprising the whole island."

Therefore, neither the unitary-state imposed on Sri Lanka during British colonial rule, nor the post-Independence constitutions left behind, reflect the realities of Lankan society.

UNITARY STATE: THE FORM OF SINHALA DOMINATION

In fact, it is a common trait in places where similar unitary states have been imposed on disparate nations by colonial powers that the majority nation uses the state to maintain its domination over smaller nations within the imposed state structure. After that, it is usually only a matter of time before national self-consciousness and the demand for self-determination arises.

The idea that Tamils are an `ethnic minority' living in a Sinhala-Buddhist country - or tenants in a Sinhala house - must be recognised as a distinctly post-Independence phenomenon that has over the years been deliberately cultivated by shrewd Sinhala politicians for opportunistic reasons.

Indeed, the last Sinhala kingdom (before it perished in the mid-19th century after the British captured it) had amicable relations with the Tamil kingdom in the North and East. And earlier, during failed military efforts by Portuguese colonialists to defeat the Sinhala kingdom, a Tamil king, Sankili, was known to have militarily helped the Sinhala king defend his territory.

Some time after, when the Sinhala royal lineage came to an abrupt end, the Sinhala aristocracy invited a Tamil prince from South India to take over. Hence, the last king of the Sinhala Kingdom who perished defending it from British invaders was a Tamil surrounded by Tamil princesses and with a Tamil queen. The Sinhala aristocracy serving this king respected the Tamil language as the medium of communication within the Royal Court and even signed various documents in Tamil. The king's faith being Hinduism seemed to have had a strong impact on the practice of Buddhism by his subjects. In Buddhist temples one would invariably find a shrine for Hindu Gods as well.

So what explains the particularly ugly brand of chauvinism found among the Sinhala people and Sinhala politicians today?

The main culprit is the system of government imposed on the country by British colonialists.

Before Independence, neither Tamil nor Sinhalese people had any notion of a unified country in the current sense. In fact, for over five centuries before Independence, both Sinhala and Tamil kingdoms evolved largely in their own way without any serious antagonism.

So `democracy', when imposed on a territory without giving due consideration to the social realities of that territory, can have disastrous consequences. That is exactly what happened when the British imposed a unitary state in Sri Lanka thereby, in effect, handing the reins of political power to the numerically bigger nation, the Sinhala nation.

Thereafter, there arose a vested interest and indeed an **incentive** on the part of competing Sinhala political parties to rally the Sinhala majority around them. And the most effective method of doing this, they found, was to whip up anti-Tamil communalism.

Thus, Mr. S.W.R.D. Bandaranayake (father of President Chandrika Kumaratunga) who in the 1920's argued for federalist self-rule for the Tamil nation, made a dramatic U-turn in the 1950's to defeat his UNP opponents by campaigning for the general election on a blatantly communalist card (epitomized in his slogan `Sinhala Only Act Within 24 Hours'). Since then, the main Sinhala political parties have found themselves engaged in a shameless race to prove to the Sinhala majority that each is more pro-Sinhala (or anti-Tamil) than the other.

It was Mr. J.R. Jayawardane, a former President of Sri Lanka, who once said in an interview to a British newspaper that the more he starved the Tamils in the North the more the Sinhalese in the South would be happy.

The Sinhala politicians' anti-Tamil campaigns began right from the time of Independence in 1948. It was the first UNP government under Mr. D.S. Senanayake which introduced the infamous Citizenship Act which dis-enfranchised hundreds of thousands of Tamils of Indian origin.

In the mid-50s, the competition between major Sinhala political parties to consolidate their support among the Sinhala electorate took a decisive turn with Mr. Bandaranayake's massive election victory in the 1956 general elections. It was an election fought purely on communalist slogans. Since then, a vicious circle was set in motion whereby Sinhala politicians, the press and the Sinhala masses inevitably got trapped in a process of reinforcing mutual chauvinistic sentiments. Even left-wing political parties involved in parliamentary politics had to betray their original principles of `parity and equality between Sinhala and Tamil nations' and jump onto the chauvinist band-wagon in order to secure Sinhala votes.

Upper-class Tamil parliamentarians who during the struggle against British colonial rule had shared a common platform with Sinhala political leaders became increasingly baffled by the monster being created by Sinhala politicians for political opportunism and they found themselves more and more discredited among the Tamil masses in the face of continuous betrayals, broken promises and outright cheating by countless Sinhala political leaders.

THE EVOLUTION OF TAMIL CONSCIOUSNESS

While Sinhala chauvinism was growing in leaps and bounds as a direct result of the political system installed by the British, Tamil national consciousness was also changing as a response to these developments in the South. These changes are clearly reflected in the shifting voting patterns of the Tamil people after Independence.

First, Tamils overwhelmingly voted for the Tamil Congress who were representatives of the unitary state. But as the anti-Tamil politics of Sinhala politicians grew steadily in the rush to impress the Sinhala electorate, the Federal Party sprang up among the Tamil masses.

The second stage of the development of Tamil national consciousness was marked by Tamil peoples' change of loyalty from the Tamil Congress to the Federal Party. But soon, Tamil people became disillusioned with federalism too as Sinhala political leaders continued to cheat them for political gains. By now Sinhala politicians had become total victims of the chauvinistic momentum they themselves had created.

The third stage in the development of Tamil national consciousness was marked by the formation of the Tamil United Liberation Front (TULF) which pledged to win independence and create the separate state of `Tamil Eelam'.

But although the leaders of the TULF paid lip-service to the creation of an independent state under growing pressure from the radicalizing Tamil masses they knew that such an aim could not be realized through a Sinhala-dominated parliament. Perhaps these leaders were trying to use the strengthening will of the Tamil people as a bargaining chip for a better deal from Sinhala politicians. So they made the demand for a separate state their main slogan in the general election of 1977.

The results of that election may be seen as the culmination of that third stage in the development of Tamil national consciousness. Here, the overwhelming majority of the Tamil people voted for a separate state thereby giving a clear democratic mandate for the TULF leadership.

But the traditional leadership was obviously not up to the task. They had no alternative strategy other than putting pressure on Sinhala leaders. And Sinhala politicians, already fully devoured by the chauvinistic vicious circle, were in no mood to compromise. Instead, they reacted by devising political manoeuvres to oust all TULF M.P.s from parliament.

Moreover, the Sinhala-dominated state began to terrorize Tamil people using physical violence in the most despicable ways, culminating in the burning to rubble of the revered Jaffna library. Meanwhile, state-sponsored colonization of the Tamil homeland, which included at times chasing out Tamil villagers and giving Sinhala names to traditional Tamil villages, was occurring at an accelerating pace.

TULF leaders had no idea how to respond to such onslaughts from the government. And their impotence soon became exposed before the Tamil masses. It was within this context that the Tamil youth began to take up arms to carry out the democratic mandate given by their people.

The Sinhala political establishment, for its part, had no choice but to abide by the ideology it had created and to mobilize its military might to crush the will of the Tamil nation. In this sense, Chandrika Kumaratunga's massive military onslaught upon Jaffna is merely the logical conclusion of the anti-Tamil momentum whipped up by her father all those years ago.

So, the main cause of the polarization of two once neighborly nations to the point of genocidal war, is the inappropriate state structure imposed on the country by the British colonialists who did not take into consideration the social realities of the island. Democracy, devoid of this consideration, leads to more harm than good.

Now that the Tamil nation has developed fully-fledged national consciousness, it is an illusion to think a `Sinhala' government in the South can ever impose a `solution' on the Tamil nation by force.

Even if government forces manage to recapture all rebel-held territories from LTTE control, it would not be long before an underground guerrilla movement emerged to challenge the government again.

Therefore, a solution can only be achieved by a voluntary agreement; and, at present, such an agreement can only be reached by acknowledging that the LTTE are the incontrovertible leaders of the Tamil liberation struggle and by withdrawing the `Sinhala' forces occupying the Tamil homeland. Any plans to marginalize the LTTE and impose a new administration under military control are doomed to fail.

FUTILITY OF PA STRATEGY

For the government to merely reveal the `package' over the LTTE's head is not going to achieve much - simply because the majority of Tamils in the North will treat this with the suspicion it deserves. After all, the `package' could well be the government's latest trick to create maximum confusion and division within the Tamil nation in its effort to crush the leaders of their liberation struggle. And if the government were ever to succeed in destroying the Tigers, the Tamil people would be completely at the government's mercy, vulnerable to whatever solution the `Sinhala' government decides to impose.

However, Tamil people, through bitter experience since 1948, have learnt to distrust all Sinhala governments, and the present government does not fare better. In fact, the PA government's `war for peace' has turned it into the most hated of all governments in the eyes of the Tamil people in general.

So the chances of the present government regaining the confidence of the Tamil people are very slim indeed. After all, a government which can go back on so many promises given to the Sinhala majority during the recent election campaign (most notably, the written assurance to abolish the Executive Presidency by the 15th of July 1995) could easily break whatever promises it gives to the Tamil people.

RADICAL CHANGE OF PERCEPTION

Meanwhile, the futility of trying to exclude the LTTE from negotiations is becoming more obvious by the day. Indeed, there needs to be a radical change in the government's perception of the Tamil liberation struggle.

The Sinhala political elite has to see the Tamil struggle as part of a global phenomenon presently raging in many parts of the world. As the General Secretary of the United Nations recently acknowledged: soon there will be 50 or so new countries on our planet.

That is the sort of struggle the `Sinhala' regime in the South has on its hands and that is why an ideological metamorphosis is necessary soon.

The Tamil struggle belongs to an unfinished global democratic revolution in which repressed nations all over the world are fighting for their fundamental rights to nationhood so that they can co-exist with other nations on an **equal** basis. It is high time the Sinhala political elite recognized this.

And they must also recognize that trying to isolate the Tigers from the Tamil people is bound to fail because the overwhelming majority of Tamils recognize the LTTE as the movement which embodies their national aspirations - aspirations that have been ruthlessly `hushed' by one Sinhala government after another.

QUEBECERS, SCOTS AND TAMILS

I would like to make a few comments about the recent referendum held in the mainly-French province of Quebec in Canada, which was aimed at gathering the French majority's verdict on the demand for separation. I understand that the people of Quebec already enjoy substantial powers of self-government and also that most of the Prime Ministers of the Canadian federal government since its formation have been of French origin.

There is a somewhat similar case in Britain, where sections within the Scottish and Welsh nations vehemently campaign for separation at every election. Substantial sections within all these nations can be seen arguing repeatedly for independence so that they might rejoin their relevant counterparts at a different level, e.g., as members of the European Union. However, thanks to the level of self-rule these nations already enjoy, the majority of people in each nation have not yet given a clear approval for separation.

Now, if one compares these cases with the situation in Sri Lanka, one can easily see the legitimacy of the Tamil struggle. Anybody with even a cursory acquaintance of the post-Independence history of Sri Lanka would agree with me when I say that **if either the French in Quebec or the Scots in Britain underwent even a fraction of the oppression the Tamil people have had to undergo in Sri Lanka, both the Canadian federation and the United Kingdom would have broken up a long time ago.**

Earlier, I said that most Canadian Prime Ministers have been of French origin. I wonder how many foreign governments know that there has **never** been a President, Prime Minister, Defence Minister or Finance Minister of Tamil origin in Sri Lanka. I wonder how many foreign governments know that Buddhism is the state religion of Sri Lanka.

How many know about the state-sponsored genocidal attacks on innocent Tamil civilians unleashed merely for the purpose of terrorizing them?

How many foreign governments know about state-sponsored Sinhala colonization of traditional Tamil homelands carried out on a massive scale purely to secure advantage for Sinhala political parties by reducing Tamils' political strength and disrupting the contiguity of their homeland?

How many foreign governments know about successive Sinhala governments having starved the Tamil homeland of capital funding thereby forcing many middle-class Tamils to migrate to Colombo for their economic well-being? (Of course, these Tamils had to face several racist attacks since the 1950's and were compelled to take refuge in the North and the East from time to time).

Unlike the French in Quebec and the Scots in Britain, Tamils voted overwhelmingly for a separate state in a general election in 1977. But, quite unlike how the governments in Ottawa and London would respond, the Colombo government reacted violently using terror methods and ruthless political maneuvers to crush the Tamils' quest for independence thereby forcing the Tamil youth to take up arms to carry out the people's mandate.

GOVERNMENT'S IDEOLOGY VERSUS REALITY

It is the failure to appreciate this reality which has set into motion the government's present naive ideology of trying to win the hearts and minds of the Tamil people without trying to win the trust of their leadership. Indeed, Sinhala politicians think `Tamil Eelam' is just a dream of Tiger `fanatics'.

Since 1983, the alienation felt by the Tamil nation has only become more and more deep-rooted. This is not surprising, given that a whole new generation has grown up entirely during the war and their only impression about the South comes from continuous bombardments and shelling by the Sinhala army.

The Tamil people, naturally, were delighted when the overwhelming majority in the South gave a clear mandate for the PA government to negotiate a settlement with the LTTE. In fact, it was the LTTE which largely mobilized people in the North to show their enthusiasm for peace in the beginning. But their enthusiasm was cut short when they realized that Sinhala politicians were again conspiring to hood-wink them.

"FOUR PILLARS" OF THE PEACE PROCESS

On the 23rd of July, 1995 a leader of the government's propaganda unit, Mr Reginald Cooray, MP, published a lengthy reply to my article in the Sunday Observer, celebrating what he called the four pillars of the government's strategy during the last peace-effort which collapsed on April 19, 1995.

This article is very revealing indeed, because it totally confirms my own interpretation of the government's intentions.

According to Mr Cooray, the four pillars of the government's peace initiative were:

(1)   Establishing a rapport with the Tamil people

(2)   A commitment to maintaining the "cessation of hostilities"

(3)   Implementing programs for rehabilitation and reconstruction

(4)   Formulating a political package

Not surprisingly, the importance of establishing a rapport with the LTTE as part of the government's strategy is not mentioned anywhere. This is no accident in my view. It betrays a lack of any commitment at all to negotiating a solution with the Tigers. (One can contrast this strategy with the `serious' efforts of peace-makers in South Africa and the Middle East). The Sri Lankan government's strategy, however, was limited to reaching the Tamil people over the head of their leadership.

My personal acquaintance with military leaders and top government layers convinced me beyond doubt that the government had totally ruled out reaching a political settlement with the LTTE very early on.

In my estimation, it was around February of 1995 that President Kumaratunga became `converted' to the military view that crushing the Tiger leadership would be a pre-condition for a political settlement with the Tamil people. And it was not long before this view became the center-piece of the government's `ideology'.

CESSATION OF HOSTILITIES VS FORMAL CEASE-FIRE

The second `pillar' of the government's strategy, i.e., its commitment to maintaining the `cessation of hostilities' does not at all contradict my interpretation of the peace process. For, given the government strategy I have outlined, it would be in its best interests to `drag' out the cessation of hostilities so it could have as much time as it needed to undermine the LTTE's mass base.

It is also not surprising that the government was reluctant to come to a `formal cease-fire' as later requested by the LTTE. The reason is obvious: a formal written cease-fire would have put irritating restrictions on the government's clandestine activities, particularly in the East. Here, Colonel Ratwatta was in full swing strengthening army bases while a new state-aided settlement was ceremoniously opened up in the highly sensitive area of Trincomallee. Also, government-sponsored Tamil mercenary groups were exploiting the `safe' atmosphere of peace talks, and eventually a prominent LTTE officer was killed by another armed Tamil group which was freely roaming about with the government's blessings.

It does not take a genius to see that the LTTE had legitimate security concerns like these. They felt insecure, and that is why they began insisting on a `formal cease-fire' arrangement.

I was in Jaffna during this period and Dr. Anton Balasingham explained to me that the LTTE thought it necessary to have a formal cease-fire at this stage. He also explained that the exact nature and conditions of activities (regarding both sides) ought to be agreed upon in **precise** terms in order to prevent further misunderstandings.

However, the government deliberately ignored the LTTE's request for a formal cease-fire. This is why the LTTE began to insist on the right of their own cadres in the East to carry arms.

With deepening suspicions about the government's motives, the LTTE wanted to settle this matter before 'substantive discussions' could start on 'political issues'. Who can blame them? It is not easy to talk politics while your opponent holds a knife at your throat.

POONERYN CAMP VERSUS SANGUPITTY ROAD

It is in this context that the 'Sangupitty Road' issue cropped up. The government tended to brush over the strategic complexity of this issue (in relation to the Pooneryn army camp) to give the impression of LTTE intransigence, but we should grapple with it more thoroughly.

The LTTE insisted on the removal of the Pooneryn army camp **before any opening up of the road**. This is understandable: Pooneryn had been occupied by the security forces during the UNP administration in order to seal the only remaining gap in the military stronghold on the Jaffna peninsula. If the LTTE had opened up their side of the Sangupitty Road whilst the Pooneryn camp remained intact they would have left themselves very vulnerable indeed.

Then what happened? Whilst the debate was raging, the government suddenly opened up its side of the Road and ordered the state media to give special publicity to this act. I can think of only one possible explanation for this 'hostile' manoeuver: it was intended to turn the Tamil people against the LTTE by making it appear as though the LTTE alone was obstructing Tamils' free access to the mainland. Aware that this was one of the harshest problems being faced by the Tamil people, the government wanted to demonise the LTTE so the people would turn against them.

The government's naivety, of course, prevented it from seeing that the Tamil nation, having clocked-up generations of experience about the unreliability and two-facedness of Sinhala governments, could easily sympathize with the LTTE's security concerns.

CROCODILE TEARS

Indeed, the empty words of heart-breaking concern for the welfare of Tamil people which effortlessly flow from the mouths of Sinhala politicians carry no weight among Tamil people. Through bitter experience, the Tamil nation has learned to recognize `crocodile tears' when they see them. And the present military occupation of the Tamil homeland by Sinhala troops has only confirmed to them the `real feelings' Sinhala politicians have towards them.

To illustrate further the hidden aim the government had during the `cessation of hostilities' let me mention one of my own experiences.

As Chairman of the National Television Network, I visited Jaffna during this period and had discussions with two senior LTTE representatives, Dr. Anton Balasingham and Mr. Thamil Chelvan, about the possibility of setting up a television studio in Jaffna so that we could transmit regular programs about developments in the North to the people in the South, at the same time as doing programs from the South for the benefit of the Tamil masses in the North. The LTTE happily agreed, I was delighted. But when I brought the message to the President she vehemently opposed the idea and instead ordered state-controlled radio (SLBC) to start programs aimed at Tamil audiences in the North.

Meanwhile, the National Television Network, Rupavahini, was asked to provide Tamil programs to the Palaly army camp in the North, to be broadcast using the army transmitter there.

Around this time, the government also launched a new military recruitment campaign using posters printed exclusively in Sinhala and distributed in selected areas in the South. Such a manoeuver would almost certainly have distressed the LTTE had they come to know about it through their intelligence network.

MILITARY RESTRUCTURING PROGRAM

Anybody who knows about the `re-structuring' program of the armed forces implemented by military leaders during the peace process can be left in no doubt as to the hidden intentions of the government.

During the previous UNP administration the military top brass wanted to capture the East from the LTTE. This was very much in line with the UNP government's political manoeuvers in that, as far as the Sinhala electorate was concerned, it was the East that has always been controversial, not the North. Hence, the military concentrated on the East.

However, there was a school of thought within the army leadership at that time which strongly believed that crushing the LTTE should be the fundamental military objective, and that the only way to achieve that was to capture Jaffna - the Tiger stronghold. They supported this tactic in the full knowledge that such an offensive would inflict enormous misery on civilians. But the protagonists of this school of thought were marginalized during the previous administration.

When the new PA government came to power the `Jaffna-targeting' strategists were brought to the forefront. President Chandrika's role, then, was to win the much-needed public support from a substantial section of the Tamil people, the Sinhala South and the international community, in order to facilitate the planned high-risk military operation.

That, I claim, was the hidden agenda of the so-called peace-process. In fact, the President did succeed in achieving that aim as far as the Sinhala South and the international community is concerned, even though she failed in driving a wedge between the Tamil people and the LTTE. She paved the way for the military leaders to carry out the new strategy which, in their view, could not be implemented under the previous regime due to half-heartedness and political opportunism (though it is also true that steps were taken during the UNP administration to place a strangle-hold on the Jaffna peninsula).

Therefore, the `second pillar' of the government's so-called `ideology' during the peace process (i.e., maintaining the cessation of hostilities) also fits very well with my interpretation of the government's hidden strategy. The Tigers' decision to pull out from negotiations at that early stage did create serious problems for the government, though in another sense it turned out to be a blessing in disguise for the President, in terms of winning public support for what is now thought of by many as the `unavoidable' war-effort.

MANIPULATING TAMIL LOYALTIES

The third component of the government's strategy, according to Mr Cooray, was its programs for rehabilitation and reconstruction in war-torn Tamil areas. In one of my earlier articles, published in the Sri Lankan Sunday Observer, I argued that the aim here was to hire Tamil labor on a mass scale, getting Tamils directly onto the government's pay-roll in the hope of changing their loyalties from the LTTE to the Colombo administration. I did not make this allegation irresponsibly. It was based on things mentioned at top government levels.

57

But nobody has to take my word for it. They only have to study closely the manner in which the reconstruction projects were to be implemented. The LTTE suggested that the work be handled by an Independent Authority represented by both sides. The government never agreed to that. How could it, when it had its own plans to undermine the LTTE?

The government wanted exclusive control over the foreign aid allocated for reconstruction work and it wanted to send a government Minister, Ratnasiri Wicremanayake, to Jaffna to supervise the project. The LTTE, clearly sensing the government's ulterior motives, would not let themselves be outsmarted. They knew how previous Tamil leaders had been outsmarted by Sinhala politicians time and time again since Independence.

So, I dispute the government's pretence that the reconstruction projects were motivated by a genuine concern for the suffering of Tamil people. In this instance, as in others, the government was consciously trying to undermine the LTTE's mass base, and treating them as subordinate provincial administrators of the central government **instead of as equals**.

I firmly believe that one underlying cause for the collapse of the peace process was the present political establishment's ideological weakness. It proved itself incapable of grasping the historical content of the Tamil struggle. It is this weakness, I believe, which accounts for the government's failure to try and develop a rapport with the LTTE even now.

While I was Rupavahini Chairman, I had a unique opportunity. I was able to observe very clearly the thinking-pattern of government circles and the military establishment in general. I am very thankful for that.

DR. UYANGODA'S OBSERVATIONS

But, I am glad to say, I am not the only one who has reached similar conclusions about the handling of the peace process. Dr. Jayadeva Uyangoda was a close advisor to the President on the ethnic issue and also one of the President's envoys sent to Jaffna to meet LTTE leaders during the latter part of the peace process. It was, in fact, during his visit to Jaffna that the LTTE released most of the prisoners of war they had been holding for a number of years. Dr. Uyangoda published an article in the May/ June 1995 issue of `Pravada' magazine under the heading, `Breakdown of Peace Talks.'

There, he openly admits that the peace process was mishandled by the government and that the LTTE's decision to pull out was a consequence of that. Dr. Uyangoda says, "Using our retrospective wisdom, we can now say that the PA government's peace initiative, as a process, was a weak one." He concludes: "Mr. Prabakharan was perhaps the first to realize this and he acted accordingly... Had there been a strong peace process in place, the past should not have repeated itself."

Then, reflecting on "the LTTE's allegation against Chandrika that by sending low level negotiating teams, she only demonstrated her arrogance as well as her lack of a serious approach to the process of talks," Dr. Uyangoda comments: "At face value... the above argument has a validity. While the LTTE negotiation team was headed by the chief of its political wing, no Minister was ever included in the government team. The latter was always headed by a non-political bureaucrat, the Secretary to the President."

Then, Dr. Uyangoda goes on as follows: "One has to ask the question: why is the LTTE apparently angered by the perceived low level nature of government negotiating teams?"

In response to that question, Dr. Uyangoda writes:

"[The answer] lies in the fact that the LTTE leaders consider themselves as rulers of a political entity of a sovereign nation. This political entity I, [Dr. Uyangoda], have called elsewhere a quasi-state. Any visitor to Jaffna in recent times... would not have failed to notice the enthusiasm with which the LTTE demonstrated all the trappings of a separate state - protocol, symbolism and all that. Mr. Thamil Chelvan, the political wing leader of the LTTE, would certainly have preferred Minister G.L. Peiris to Secretary Balapatabendi, to be his counterpart at the negotiating table, not necessarily because he was impatiently waiting to discuss complex constitutional problems involving the political package, but because he viewed a Minister's presence as a proper demonstration of state to `state' protocol."

He continues: "On my return from Jaffna in February this year, I told many of my friends in Colombo that the LTTE was keen not only about the substance of talks, but also of the symbolism and drama inherent in the exercise. The LTTE wanted not only a settlement with honor, but also a path that assured them of the recognition of their own sense of dignity and honor, arising from their being rulers and defenders of a nationality group. Yet, the LTTE being the LTTE, and the government being the government, this issue was never resolved."

FAILURE TO RELATE TO LTTE

I quite agree with Dr. Uyangoda's analysis here. But, my point is that the government, being incapable of understanding the content of the Tamil struggle, could not begin to relate to the LTTE in an appropriate manner.

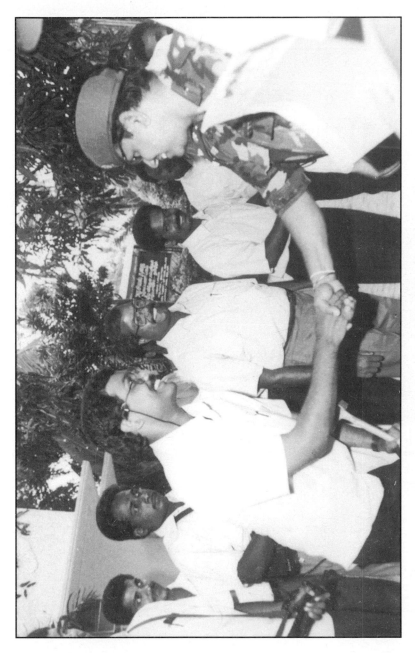

Head of the LTTE's negotiating team, Mr. Thamil Chelvan (left) greets a member of the government's team (in military gear) during peace talks

Government's negotiating team led by the President's Secretary, Mr. Balapatabandige and the LTTE team led by Mr. Thamil Chelvan, outside the LTTE conference hall in Jaffna

Dr. Jayadeva Uyangoda (left), Vasudeva Nanayakkara M.P. (far left) and other delegates from the South holding talks with Tiger leaders at the LTTE headquarters in Jaffna

The author Vasantha-Rajah with President Chandrika Kumaratunga: he had unique access to inner government circles during the peace process, prior to his resignation from the state television network

64

The President wanted to treat them as a somewhat mischievous (and subordinate) bunch of administrators - nothing more. She soon realized, however, that they were not the `pushovers' she thought they were.

Dr. Uyangoda, too, seems to have understood, albeit in retrospect, that by "peace," the two sides meant two different things. This is what he says: "They were negotiating for `peace', peace here remaining an abstract concept, an undefined notion. When they were forced by circumstances to concretise the concept, the competing perspectives became abundantly clear."

Then, Dr. Uyangoda tries to explain what the LTTE would have meant: "For [the LTTE], a peace process that did not accommodate their status of being a politico-military entity representing a sovereign nation, would not be a worthy exercise." Then, he concludes, "Throughout the peace process, these competing perceptions of the goal constituted the basis for almost all disagreements between the two sides."

Dr. Uyangoda is quite right, except that he did not realize that by then Colonel Ratwatta and some other military leaders were able to convert the President to a different strategy, by showing that the Tigers are not the sort of people she thought they were. Once the President became convinced about this, she gave her blessings for the `hidden strategy' promoted by the likes of Colonel Ratwatta.

SCHIZOPHRENIC BEHAVIOR SYMPTOMATIC

So, the government's increasingly schizophrenic behavior, ably noted by Dr. Uyangoda, was, I argue, not due to lack of professionalism or misunderstanding, but a symptom of that hidden strategy.

Coming from a man the President sent to Jaffna, Dr. Uyangoda's next statement is both astonishing and revealing. He says: "The LTTE had a fairly convincing argument for the removal of the Pooneryn Army Camp which was established in 1992 under the UNP regime, as part of a military strategy to encircle the Jaffna peninsula. If Chandrika was genuinely for peace, why can't she prove her good faith by removing just one camp from the North? asked the LTTE."

At this point, Dr. Uyangoda betrays his ignorance of Colonel Ratwatta's military strategy being cooked up with the President's blessings. He continues: "The Sri Lankan state was not yet ready to take such a bold step [as removing the Pooneryn camp]. [The President's] April 12 letter to Mr. Prabakharan contained [the] compromise... `we will review your demands of a military nature in three months.'" But, Dr. Uyangoda writes, "Mr. Prabakharan was not in a mood to make compromises."

And quite rightly, in my view. For, after sensing what the military was up to, three months would have been a fatally long time.

LANGUAGE OF NEGOTIATIONS

Since resigning from my position at Rupavahini, I have been at pains to show that during the peace process the Sri Lankan government never totally broke away from the Sinhala-chauvinist ideology that has characterized all past attempts to solve the `Tamil Question'. Dr. Uyangoda has another example which confirms this: "At one point, the LTTE reacted angrily to the language of negotiations, when the President used the term `concessions' to describe the lifting of the economic embargo." Dr. Uyangoda justifies the LTTE's anger, saying:

66

"I, for one, found myself sympathetic to the LTTE's point of view on this specific matter, and needless to say I hardly had the clout to change the terminology preferred by the government. My own position on the issue is that President Kumaratunga should never have used the idiom of the Sinhala state."

Further down in his article, Dr. Uyangoda has this to say about the lifting of the economic embargo on the North:

"[Right up to the 19th of April], the whole scene of lifting bans and prohibitions remained quite unsatisfactory on the ground and it had actually irked the LTTE. Even the government's decision to lift the ban on fishing in the North and Eastern Sea could not be properly implemented. The free transport of diesel and petrol, after lifting the ban, occurred only for 2 to three days, and that too after the Sinhala-Hindu New Year [i.e., April 14th]."

Although we must be grateful to Dr. Uyangoda for sharing his reflections, I do not think he ever realized that while he was in Jaffna, trying to convince the LTTE to drop their demand to remove the Pooneryn camp, the government was hatching its war preparations for the inevitable military show-down it expected at some point during future negotiations.

LTTE'S PULL-OUT

There are those who think that the LTTE was taking the government for a ride, but I dispute that. If that was the case, it would have been in the LTTE's interest to hold on to peace talks much longer to obtain the maximum benefit from the lifting of the economic embargo and to carry out other preparations.

67

What actually happened was that the LTTE decided to pull out rather abruptly, even at the cost of jeopardizing its image internationally. My guess is that their intelligence sources prompted them to do so, without waiting another three months as the President suggested.

The LTTE's dramatic pull-out from talks and the sudden blowing up of two Navy gun-boats did baffle the government and the military. Colonel Ratwatta, I believe, was then forced to put together his `Operation Leap Forward' rather prematurely.

To that extent, the LTTE's move was very smart. It managed to disrupt the government's agenda by putting the military off-balance.

WAR AND ECONOMY

Now, I would like to offer a serious note of caution. If the government fails to realize in time the gravity of the mistake it has made and if it fails to take immediate steps to withdraw its troops from the North it will find itself dragged deeper and deeper into an economically unaffordable war which will have disastrous implications.

Indeed, the government is already facing huge problems with the electorate in the South mainly because of the difficulty in delivering major election promises. Until recently, it has been attempting to divert attention from these other important issues citing the war as an excuse. But that cannot work for long.

On the political front, the government has bluntly backed-off from its promise to abolish the Executive Presidency. On the welfare front, it has failed to introduce the promised unemployment benefit and the family allowance for the poor. On the economic front, it has failed to create the 500, 000 jobs it promised within one year.

All these splintered promises are contributing to the build-up of social tensions in the South. And it goes without saying that getting bogged down further in a costly war will be fatal for the government. As Adrian Wijemanna, political analyst and writer on the ethnic problem, points out: "the Sri Lankan government simply does not have the means to win this war." Mr. Wijemanna has made a striking comparison:

"[In terms of troops], the Sri Lankan government field ten to one against the LTTE; the British failed to defeat the IRA in Northern Ireland with 100 to 1 against them. The Sri Lankan government spends 29 billion rupees per year on the war; the British government spent nearly ten times that amount per year on a much smaller war without success. Even if the Sri Lankan government spends 10 times what it now spends per year, it will not be enough, as it faces a far greater challenge than the British faced in Northern Ireland. Even if civil government among the Sinhala people is replaced by a military dictatorship and all the programs of civil government are scrapped leaving only the barest minimum required for the war-effort, there will still not be enough foreign-exchange for the imported military hardware required for an expanded military effort. The USA and Britain, both far richer countries than Sri Lanka and both manufacturers of all the military hardware required for their war-efforts, failed to overcome nationalist guerrillas fighting on their home ground in Vietnam and Northern Ireland. Sri Lanka is one of the poorest countries; the LTTE is the most formidable guerilla force in the world. It is not possible for the Sri Lankan government militarily to exterminate them. The LTTE is as permanent a feature on the island as the Sri Lankan army."

I think Mr. Wijemanna's analysis and warnings must be taken very seriously indeed.

WHITHER PA?

I have my own concerns about the future if the government fails to make drastic changes in its present approach to the Tamil problem.

Its much-trumpeted `free-media' policy will continue to slide backwards as the climate of paranoia and insecurity deepens. Indeed, the whole social climate is likely to darken: instability, fear, economic chaos and social unrest could well become the order of the day.

A continued war would also further jeopardize the government's economic strategy, and it is an all-too-real possibility that ultra-rightist Sinhala elements will campaign to bring a military junta to power. Some tabloid newspapers have already begun such a campaign.

In order to achieve a just and lasting peace the Government of Sri Lanka has to show sincerity towards the Tamil people, and that means: stop the war, withdraw all troops and re-enter into negotiations with the leadership of the Tamil struggle, the Liberation Tigers of Tamil Eelam.

I had the opportunity (or misfortune) of seeing a video that was recently smuggled out of Jaffna and has now reached London. It exposes the most horrifying scenes of civilian casualties caused by indiscriminate aerial bombing and shelling in the North. After seeing those scenes, I could imagine how ordinary Tamil people would respond to the government's devolution package.

But the government seems hell-bent on continuing its war-strategy in the North, thus alienating the Tamil people even further from the South.

AN EYE-WASHER

Even well before the invasion of Jaffna, one Tamil community leader in London, commenting on the devolution package, said: "This central government, with Buddhism as the state religion, can only be conceived as a Sinhala-Buddhist government. Therefore, the limited powers devolved to the regions are an eye-washer to hold on to Sinhalese dominance over the Tamil nation; and we shall not be fooled by that." But, he said, "it could be used as a starting point for further negotiations if the government is serious. We don't think the government is sincere; we think it's merely a mask to invade the Tamil homeland."

And even prior to `Operation Sunshine' the parliamentary Opposition and Buddhist High Priests had declared their opposition to the package. The government knew it could not get the 2/3 majority in parliament and approval of the Sinhala majority in a referendum for the package in its original form. President Chandrika requested them not to rock the boat until the war was concluded. In other words, she gave the `nod and the wink' that once the LTTE is crushed the government can impose a diluted version of the package without much resistance. In the aftermath of the capture of Jaffna, the dilution process is already underway.

REALITY OF LTTE RULE

I want at this point to emphasize the importance of understanding the reality of LTTE rule and the respect the Tamil people have developed towards their leaders. Since the LTTE came to power, it has implemented a range of impressive social measures that the Tamil people have come to appreciate.

The widespread slaughter of goats for religious sacrifice is no longer permitted. According to tradition, 20 to 30 goats used to be dragged into temples on special occasions and their necks cut as an offering to God. But the LTTE has convinced the Tamil people that such cruelty to animals is unnecessary and evil and the practice no longer takes place.

DOWRY AND CASTE

The dowry system, which used to benefit only a minority of well-off people and which oppressed many poor women, was banned by the LTTE. Also, the caste-system, which was a deep-rooted social institution that led to a great deal of hardship and inhumane treatment of low-caste communities, was outlawed because it was seen as an instrument of social oppression.

In the past, a man from a low-caste could not even enter a temple or marry a high-caste girl. Now, if the same man falls in love with a girl from a high-caste, and if they wish to marry, they can do so without any problems. Earlier, a socially powerful high-caste family could unleash terror on the low-caste lover with the full support of the police. But now, the LTTE `community police' and courts of law protect the low-caste poor against such oppression and, meanwhile, a low-caste person can enter a temple and worship God without any restrictions.

These examples further undermine the image painted of the LTTE as a bunch of fanatics who have no regard for the welfare of the Tamil people. Mere opportunists could not make such bold and progressive leaps.

ENVIRONMENT AND WELFARE

The LTTE has also banned the felling of trees because they realized that if the practice continued unchallenged, much long-term environmental damage would be incurred. Indeed, to encourage `environment-friendly' attitudes, on special national occasions they distribute plants to every family so that people can plant a tree in their garden as a symbolic gesture.

In spite of their massive military responsibilities the LTTE never shirks its responsibilities in helping the poor through social services. For example, a poor child no longer has to give up education because he or she is poor. In the old days, many poor children had to give up studies and do laboring work to contribute to their domestic finances. But the LTTE has taken steps to help such children. If a poor student has financial difficulties, a bank account is opened in that student's name so that he or she can use the money deposited in that account for educational expenses.

What this demonstrates is that the LTTE cannot be characterized merely as selfish terrorists whose only concern is war and their own survival. On the contrary, they clearly exhibit qualities of good leadership with genuine concern for their people. The greatly exaggerated information from dubious sources of a `reign of terror' only creates a false impression of the situation that leads to misconceived strategies such as the government is pursuing now.

LTTE police march at a parade

Front-view of LTTE's Jaffna police station before the city was overrun by the 'Sinhala' army

LTTE police women at work within LTTE-held territory

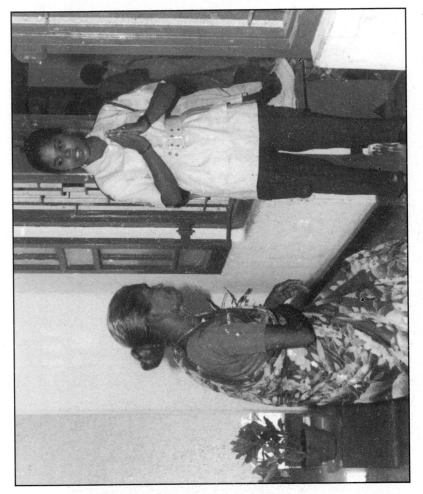

An LTTE police woman greets an old woman entering the police station

A case being heard in a Jaffna court - within the LTTE's de facto government

Interior of a play center provided by the LTTE administration

A sports meet held in a girl's school under war conditions in LTTE territory

POLITICAL MATURITY

The LTTE is a politically mature leadership with a global vision. Recently, I asked one leader of its International Secretariat, Mr. Murali, "What is your dream for mankind as a whole?" His answer impressed me: "I would love to see the day when there is `one world', with no national boundaries, and the whole of mankind can share the wealth of the world fairly. But to achieve that goal, first there should not be any nation being oppressed by another. So, the Tamil national struggle is only a step towards achieving that goal. We are not narrow-minded nationalists. Our nationalism is an `enlightened' nationalism which does not contradict internationalism."

This answer from Mr. Murali surprised me. It showed me that he was not a narrow-minded nationalist fanatic but a sensible man with a noble vision whose views have advanced far beyond many so-called `liberals' who criticize the Tamil liberation struggle as the work of a few `backward fanatics'.

SOME UNFAIR CRITICISMS

Many historians have (albeit sometimes indirectly) glorified historic events such as the French Revolution, the American Revolution and many other freedom struggles in history, regardless of the extreme atrocities and violence which occurred as a result of those conflicts. In a similar sense, the Tamil liberation struggle must also be seen as essentially progressive and historically justifiable.

The much-criticized phenomenon of young kids joining the armed struggle, though not very palatable to most of us, should not surprise anybody who has seen similar struggles in the Middle East, the Far East and Africa which have dragged on for many years breeding entire generations of youth totally under war conditions.

81

Author in discussion with the leader of the LTTE's Swiss branch, Mr. Murali

Recently, I met a nineteen year old LTTE member in Zurich who told me that he joined the Tigers when he was 13 years of age. I asked if he was forced to join the Tigers to which he laughed and replied "Oh no, my brother and my father were killed by the Sinhala army, and after that I willingly joined the Tigers". He had come to Europe to get treatment for a serious injury and was eagerly waiting to return to the battle-front in the North.

The much-feared phenomena of Black Tigers, suicide-squads and cadres wearing cyanide capsules etc., can also, I think, be explained in terms of the strength of the will-power generated under particular historical circumstances; and, I do not think such phenomena are exceptional to the Liberation Tigers; nor are they symptomatic of any perverse attachment to death and destruction.

A point raised by LTTE leader, Mr. V. Prabhakaran, in a recent message sent to a rally organized by several political parties in Tamil Nadu, may be of relevance in this regard:

Referring to an incident where a Muslim youth in Tamil Nadu had burnt himself to death in protest against the Sri Lankan government's military adventure in Jaffna, Mr. Prabhakaran appealed: "We are deeply saddened to note a recent incident in Trichi where a youth has taken his life by self-immolation as an extreme form of expression of solidarity. While we pay our respects to his passion for freedom and his sentiments of ethnic love, we feel that such acts of self-sacrifice are unnecessary and, therefore, have to be avoided". [The full text of this message is printed in the appendix]

The LTTE leader's response can be usefully contrasted with the enthusiastic encouragement given by Buddhist clergy to acts of self-immolation carried out by Buddhist monks in Saigon in the 60's. Does Mr. Prabakaran's appeal sound at all like that of a fanatic hell-bent on killing and destruction?

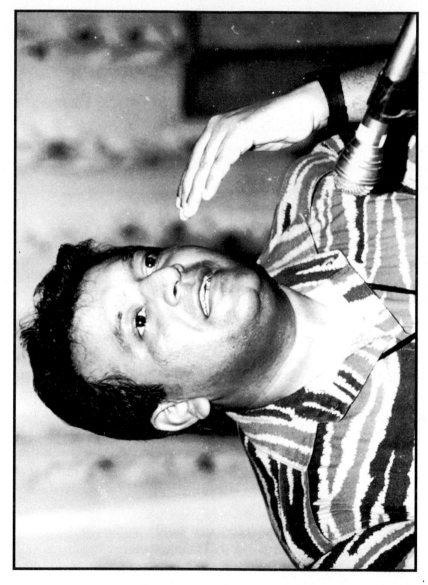

LTTE leader, Mr. V. Prabhakaran, addresses a meeting

Indeed, many of the widely peddled criticisms against the Liberation Tigers have only helped to prevent outsiders from understanding the real nature of the Tamil struggle and its leadership.

What is closer to the truth is that the LTTE is respected greatly by the Tamil people and that any attempt to drive a wedge between the two is doomed to fail. The only way of building trust with the Tamil people is to re-start sincere negotiations with their leaders with a view to coming to a just settlement which respects Tamils' right to self-determination.

So, I reiterate: if the government wants to achieve a lasting solution, it should withdraw Sinhala troops from Tamil areas, invite the LTTE back to the discussion process **without conditions** and there must be a genuine will this time to treat them as the leaders of the Tamil people.

SINHALA AND MUSLIM COUNCILS IN THE EAST

Even though the LTTE may agree on the need to protect the rights of Sinhala and Muslim communities living in the East, it is highly unlikely they would accept the government's proposal to re-demarcate the boundaries in the Welioya area, dividing the Tamil region into two. Tamils have not forgotten that just over a decade ago these areas consisted of Tamil villages which were demolished by chasing out Tamils, in some cases even killing Tamil villagers. They were later turned into Sinhala settlements as part of government-led colonization programs in the East. In fact, `Welioya' was formerly known by the Tamil name `Manal Aru'.

Quite apart from this gruesome past, it would be very difficult for the government to justify such a carve-up when there are Tamil communities concentrated in specific areas in the South as well. (Already the leader of the Tamil workers in the up-country plantations, Mr. Thondaman, can be heard demanding a separate region for the up-country Tamils of Indian origin).

The government's determination to keep Trincomallee under its control could also become a sticking point, as the Tamils tend to see it as one of their main cities, if not **the** main city. At a time when (thanks to new technology) creating artificial, high-quality harbors anywhere is not a huge problem, I see no reason why the government should make a big fuss about it for chauvinistic reasons.

My personal view is that North and East should be merged and recognized as the Tamil homeland, while `Sinhala/ Muslim enclaves' within the Tamil state and `Tamil/ Muslim enclaves' within the Sinhala state may be granted local administrative powers with guarantees of basic rights.

However, I do not believe that the traditional political parties in the South are capable of seeing the problem in this light. Yet, as I have said, a substantial change in perception can be seen emerging within the rapidly radicalizing left-wing political spectrum in the South, which makes me increasingly optimistic about the future.

ADVICE TO THE WEST

Western governments at present seem to perceive national liberation struggles, which are raging in many parts of the world and challenging post-war national boundaries, as disruptive forces. So instead of helping the relevant states find constructive solutions to their unresolved national questions, the West has taken a negative approach by supporting the relevant governments' military efforts to crush national liberation struggles.

This is an extremely short-sighted approach which is having disastrous implications for the world-order in general and the well-being of the relevant countries in particular. Western nations obviously have not forgotten about their own struggles for independence (and for the right to self-determination) which roared in the West just a few centuries ago. What they must realize is that the national struggles which have now emerged in many Third World countries and former Communist regimes are instances of an unfinished democratic revolution they themselves began.

This does not mean that contemporary national liberation struggles have to go through the same processes that the Western nations went through. On the contrary, at a time when a strong tendency to supersede the limitations of the nation-state and to experiment with new integrated state-forms is emerging, particularly in Europe, I see no reason why the international community cannot help war-torn countries achieve imaginative solutions to their `national questions' instead of helping one side of the conflict crush the other.

IMAGINATIVE SOLUTIONS

It is a monumental error to think that high-tech warfare can put an end to powerful historical forces, unless we are prepared to wipe out entire nations. Grasping their historical inevitability and searching for imaginative solutions would pay off in the long run. If Western governments fail to realize this and if they continue to help the war-efforts of governments like Sri Lanka's, they too will have to share the responsibility (along with international arms-dealers) for causing enormous human misery and bringing financial ruin to many countries.

Considering the political maturity of the Tamil nationalist movement, Sri Lanka has a unique opportunity to experiment with unprecedented solutions to its national conflict, lighting the way forward for similar conflicts raging across the globe.

But is the Sinhala political establishment in Sri Lanka capable of achieving the ideological metamorphosis necessary to understand the Tamil struggle?

And will the Sinhala government accept the LTTE's legitimate demand to withdraw all Sinhalese forces from the Tamil homeland, before any future negotiations begin?

Unfortunately, I am becoming increasingly pessimistic about the capability of the traditional political establishment in the South to solve the Tamil problem.

TAMIL NADU FACTOR

However, political developments within Tamil Nadu and the Sinhala South will, I predict, play a significant role in helping the Tamil nation win its legitimate rights in the near future.

Recently, a general strike led by all major political parties in Tamil Nadu (including the ruling party) brought the entire state of Tamil Nadu to a **complete** standstill. This was launched in support of the Tamil struggle in Sri Lanka and it called upon the Indian central government to condemn the Colombo government's war-effort. All indications are that there is a gathering momentum in sight and the people of Tamil Nadu could prove a powerful ally for the Liberation Tigers in the near future.

But the decisive factor, in my view, will be the military, political and economic disaster confronting the Colombo administration as a direct result of the government's latest military offensive. This adventure has, ironically, contributed to the consolidation of the Tamil struggle and has pushed it into a qualitatively new stage. The Tamil exodus of some half a million people has decisively tilted the balance of forces in favor of the LTTE.

Hoisting the `Sinhala' flag in the City of Jaffna has only provided an extra impetus for thousands of Tamil youth to join the LTTE. Meanwhile, ordinary Tamil people at home and abroad have mobilized themselves around the Tiger leadership as never before. This is only to be expected because Tamils do realize now that the situation in Sri Lanka is so polarized that there is now no room for `middle-ground': either you are with the Tamil liberation struggle or you are on the government's side to crush that struggle.

The so-called `middle ground' is increasingly being seen by most Tamils as fertile ground to produce stooges for the government's Machiavellian tactics to impose its own `solution' on the Tamil people.

ANTI-CLIMAX

The climax of the government's military efforts to crush the Tamil struggle, I believe, has now passed. This is the maximum the Sinhala government can do to maintain its hegemony over the Tamil people, short of outright genocide. The anti-climax has already begun.

The LTTE will continue to paralyse supply routes from the South to Sinhalese troops `trapped' in the peninsula, by attacking planes and ships. It will also continue to attack military and economic targets in the South.

Moreover, the Liberation Tigers will in all probability develop friendly links with progressive forces in the Sinhala-South **who recognize and support Tamils right to self-determination**.

Maintaining a massive force in the North will be an enormously costly affair for the government and it is the oppressed masses in the South who will have to bear the brunt.

But the government cannot continue to rely for mass support on chauvinistic sentiments alone - for long. Indeed, we can anticipate serious socio-political upheavals in the South in the near future. The growing labor and student unrest in the immediate aftermath of the so-called military victory over the LTTE can be seen as a prelude to that.

SINHALA-SOUTH FACTOR

Recent signals coming from progressive forces in the South are extremely encouraging and significant. Already there are important developments which suggest a break-through within a substantial section of the radical political spectrum in the South who **unconditionally** oppose the war and support the Tamil struggle.

Indeed, there are political forces in the South who think that the liberation of oppressed masses in the South is **inseparably linked** to the liberation of the Tamil nation from the clutches of Sinhala domination.

It is worth noting that some of the most non-chauvinistic elements within the Sinhala-South are emerging from within this radical political spectrum. Their thinking shows a marked difference from the chauvinistic stance adopted by the radical youth movement, the JVP, which led an unsuccessful anti-government rebellion in the late 1980s.

I had lengthy discussions with one LTTE leader, the late `Kittu', who was in London during that period. He told me: "If the JVP is ready to rid itself of its chauvinistic attributes and come to an alliance with us we can open up an entire forest for them to use as both a refuge and a military training ground."

Fortunately for the then government of President Premadasa the JVP failed to make the change and consequently the link-up with the LTTE did not materialize.

President Premadasa shrewdly used this failure to his advantage by starting peace talks with the LTTE and utilizing that breathing space to mobilize his security forces in the South to crush the JVP.

LTTE's martyred leader, Col. Sathasivam Krishnakumar ('Kittu'), who took his own life to escape capture by the Indian navy

Now that a substantial section of this radical movement in the South seems to be firmly committed to the principle of Tamils' right of self-determination, there is a real possibility of a friendly link-up emerging between the two.

Such a link-up, in my view, could effectively put an end to any future efforts by the government to hood-wink Tamil and Sinhala oppressed people alike by starting bogus peace talks with the Tamil rebels while the military takes care of social upheavals in the South.

For my part, I have totally lost confidence in the ability of UNP or SLFP governments to solve the Tamil problem. I have also lost confidence in Western governments' resolve to achieve a **just** solution in Sri Lanka. Their over-riding interest seems to be protecting a government which freely allows them to exploit economic resources at will.

EMERGING POLITICAL ALLIANCES

Whether the Tamil nation in Sri Lanka has any **real** friends other than the masses in Tamil Nadu, and the emerging progressive forces in the Sinhala South, remains to be seen. One possibility is the strengthening of support from the Muslim community and the estate workers in the up-country as a result of growing Sinhala chauvinism against all Tamil-speaking communities.

One must not under-estimate the existing support for the Tamil struggle among the estate workers, reflected in the constant lip-service given to the LTTE by their leader, Mr S. Thondaman, in spite of his ministerial position within the government.

The estate workers Mr. Thondaman represents were brought from South India by the British during colonial rule to work on the tea estates. Ever since, an acute antagonism has existed between these workers and the Sinhalese communities that were displaced by their arrival, culminating in recurrent attacks against the workers. In the present climate of excessive Sinahala chauvinism, the frequency of such attacks is certain to increase and this will in all probability drive these workers to identify more and more with the aspirations of the Tamil liberation movement in general. One LTTE leader has mentioned to me that these workers would be welcome to settle in Tamil Eelam once it is established.

The Tamil-speaking Muslim community will also be affected by the renewed tide of Sinhala chauvinism and many in this community must already be feeling nervous about their own future as a minority living under a regime that is becoming increasingly chauvinistic. Perhaps LTTE theoretician Dr. Anton Balasingham's recent reply to a journalist's question about the "forceful eviction of Muslims from the North by the LTTE" may be seen as a friendly nod towards the Muslim community. Answering the question, Dr. Balasingham has said: "It was an unfortunate affair and we apologize. But there was communal tension and we asked them to leave the place without doing any harm to them. It was a mistake. We have told them that they have an inalienable right to live in peace in the North and East. Once normalcy is restored, they can return to their homes." [Delhi-based journal, `Outlook']

It is difficult to say how far this would appease the Muslim community, but there are growing signs of the Muslim young generation being attracted to the LTTE's struggle against Sinhala racism.

My guess is that as the depth of the Tamil struggle becomes more fully appreciated and as the government's high hopes of victory are dashed there is a good possibility of a powerful political alliance being forged between radical movements in Tamil Nadu and the South of Sri Lanka, and the Liberation Tigers.

In particular, the formation of an alliance between the Sinhala South and the Liberation Tigers would mark one of the most significant political developments in South Asia this century - for there have been no cases yet of a liberation struggle of a minority nation linking up with progressive forces within the majority nation with which it is at war.

****

APPENDICES

Appendix i.

University of Jaffna, Sri Lanka

Dr. Boutros Boutros-Gali
Secretary General UNO
U.N. Headquarters
New York, U.S.A.

University of Jaffna, Sri Lanka
Faculty of Agriculture,
Kilinochchi.

28 November 1995

Your Excellency,

It is with a deep sense of sorrow and pain of mind that we, the academic community of the University of Jaffna, address this letter to you to bring to your notice the immense human suffering caused by the current military operation code-named 'Operation Sunshine' by the Sri Lankan security forces in the Jaffna peninsula and to request you to intervene in a more effective way to alleviate the suffering of the affected people. We also appeal to you to pressurise the Sri Lankan government to change its hostile attitude and cause it to halt the aggressive military operations which in spite of the government's claim to the contrary, is clearly directed against the Tamil people as a whole.

Since the latest military operation began on the 17th of October in the most fertile and thickly populated areas of Valigamam East, extensive damage has been done to the lives and properties of the people in the peninsula through indiscriminate and intensive mortar and artillery shelling and bombing and wanton destruction of civilian properties by bulldozers and tanks. Many innocent people have been killed in a gruesome manner and many more have been seriously injured.

If lives have not been lost or people have not been injured on an even larger scale it is not because of the sensitivity and concern shown by the security forces for the safety of innocent civilians but because of the precaution taken by the people in evacuating quickly from areas where intense shelling and bombing were taking place and seeking shelter elsewhere. On some days shells virtually rained on civilian areas. The people in the Valigamam and Jaffna town areas have eventually been forced to flee en masse abandoning their dwellings and hard-earned belongings due to intense and indiscriminate shelling of the areas by the security forces. They have been rendered destitute overnight. Nearly five lakhs of people are now languishing as refugees, about three and a half lakhs in the Vadamaratchy and Thenmaratchy areas and the balance in the Vanni districts of Kilinochchi, Mannar, Mullaitivu and Vavuniya without proper food, shelter and sanitation. Some of the areas in Vadamaratchy, Thenmaratchy and Mullaitivu which are heavily populated by displaced people have also now come under intense shelling and aerial bombing resulting in a number of deaths and injuries to civilians. As a result, the exodus of people to comparatively safer areas in the Vanni is still continuing. We now learn that the government has reimposed a ban on travel through the Jaffna lagoon to frustrate the efforts of the people to seek shelter in a safe area.

Educational institutions in the entire North have ceased to function as students and teachers are also displaced and schools have been converted into refugee camps. Even the University of Jaffna has suspended its academic activities and has temporarily shifted to Chavakachcheri and Kilinochchi from where it is carrying out its administrative functions. All economic activities including agriculture and fishing have come to a standstill as a result of this major calamity and people need assistance on a large scale to restart their lives. Shortage of cash in the banks that are functioning has aggravated the problem further. Above all, the security of the people even in the displaced areas, is not guaranteed due to continued aerial bombing and shelling. What causes us great pain of mind is the government's unholy claim that this military operation is being

97

carried out to liberate the Tamils from the clutches of the LTTE and that the civilian casualties during the military operations are minimal. There is no record to show that the Tamils living in the North and East ever made a request to government to liberate them from the LTTE. The majority of the Tamils in fact consider the LTTE as their liberators.

The hypocrisy of the government's claim has long been exposed when it reimposed and tightened the economic embargo and severely restricted the flow of food, medicine and other essential items to the North and stopped the delivery of mail to the North besides embarking on a series of military operations causing the death of hundreds of civilians and inflicting serious injuries to thousands. Even the displacement of half a million people from their homes and the resultant large-scale human suffering has not stirred the conscience of the government, for it rushed to prevent any NGOs giving assistance to the people directly, while not taking any timely action itself to grant relief to the affected people. The government seems to have succeeded in preventing the international community and even some fair-minded Sinhalese in the South from knowing the actual extent of the hardship caused to the civilian population in the North-East by the military operations, through false propaganda and press censorship and by refusing to grant permission for independent observers to travel to the war-affected areas in the North and East. Any person who attempts to give the correct picture of the situation is branded and harassed by the government as a 'terrorist' or a 'terrorist' supporter.

The history of the Tamils in Sri Lanka and genesis and aggravation of the ethnic conflict is too well known and need no recapitulation here. However, it is pertinent to point out that the Tamils have ruled themselves for several centuries and have also ruled over other regions of Sri Lanka. Jaffna has remained a vibrant cultural, educational and commercial centre of the Tamils from time immemorial and was the capital of the Jaffna Kingdom. Tamils and the Sinhalese were brought under a single polity only after the advent of the British rule. When the British left the shores of Sri Lanka power passed into the hands of the Sinhalese who because of their overwhelming ethnic majority were able to consolidate their power to the detriment of the Tamil community. Tamils were discriminated against in the spheres of education, employment, language use and land use. Tamil areas were systematically colonised by Sinhalese people with state aid with a view to breaking the contiguity of the Tamil homeland and rendering the Tamils weak politically and economically. The suppression by military means of all forms of non-violent and democratic agitations by the Tamils against these discriminations led to the birth and growth of militancy among the Tamils which was met by further state terrorism and communal violence by the Sinhalese against the Tamil people. Tamils have now been completely alienated from the mainstream of Sri Lankan politics. The present government by its activities has helped communalism to raise its ugly head again in the South on an unprecedented scale. No part of Sri Lanka is now safe for the Tamils to live. After the recent events there is hardly any Tamil in the North and East who thinks that a settlement of the ethnic problem under a single Sri Lankan polity is desirable or possible. The current military operation has only strengthened the resolve of the Tamils to continue to fight to regain their status as a separate nation so that they can look after their own affairs without being subjected to the tyranny of an ethnic majority.

As people who have been rendered destitute ourselves overnight along with lakhs of other civilians by the military operation of the Sri Lankan security forces we appeal to you to use your good offices to:

1. impress upon the Sri Lankan government to halt its military operation and withdraw its armed forces from the occupied areas so that the displaced people can return to their homes.

2. arrange for an immediate cease-fire and resumption of talks between the government and the LTTE.

3. persuade the government to lift the economic embargo imposed on the people in the North.

4. provide relief and assistance to the affected people direct through the NGOs until such time as the government lifts the economic embargo, for a government which continues to impose the economic embargo cannot be expected to act fairly in the matter of distribution of aid for relief.

5. provide assistance to people who wish to settle down in the Vanni district permanently.

6. pressurise the government to allow the local and foreign press and other observers to visit the North and make an independent assessment of the present situation.

7. render all other possible assistance to enable the people in the North to re-start their educational and other activities and lead a normal life with self-respect and dignity without being driven to a permanent refugee status in their own homeland.

8. to bring pressure on the government to lift the ban on travel through the Jaffna lagoon which is the only safe route available at present to the affected Tamils to move to safer areas in the mainland.

Yours truly,

Name	Designation
Prof. K.Kunaratnam	Senior Professor of Physics
Prof.S.V. Parameswaran	Senior Professor of Physiology

Prof. S.Mageswaran	Senior Professor of Chemistry
Dr. A. Navaratnarajah	Senior Lecturer in Animal Science
Dr. S.Mohanadas	Senior Lecturer in Agricultural Chemistry
Mr. S.Rajadurai	Senior Lecturer in Agronomy
Mrs. R. Pararajasingham	Librarian
Prof. A. Sanmugadas	Professor of Tamil
Mr. R.Vijararatnam	Senior Lecturer in Agricultural Engineering
Dr. C.S. Nachinarkinian	Senior Lecturer in Community Medicine
Dr. K. Sivapalan	Senior Lecturer in Physiology
Mr. R.Nanthakumaran	Senior Lecturer in Economics
Miss. S.Arulanantham	Assistant Librarian
Miss. K. Thirunavukarasu	Assistant Librarian
Mr. S.Thevathasan	Senior Staff Officer (Statistics)
Mr. K.Parameswaran	Registrar U/J
Prof. P. Balasundarampillai	Dean/Arts
Prof. N. Balakrishnan	Professor in Economics
Mr. Antony Rajan	Lecturer in Geography
Dr. K. Kugabalan	Senior Lecturer in Geography

Appendix ii.

Inter-Religious Union of Jaffna
115, Fourth cross street, Jaffna, Sri Lanka

The Secretary General,   Temporary Address:
United Nations Organisation,   H. F Convent
U. N. Headquarters,   Mirusuvil,
New York U. S. A   Sri Lanka.

                                        17 November 1995

Dear Sir,

The ongoing war in the Jaffna peninsula, we are sure, has already engaged your attention. We are certain that as the most important Organisation in the world for the formation of justice and peace among countries and nationalities, you will want to exert your good influence to restore justice and peace among the nationalities in Sri Lanka. We thank you, on behalf of the people of Jaffna, for the moving appeal you already made to the various organisations of the world to rush humanitarian assistance to the nearly half a million Tamils made refugees in their own homeland.

As religious leaders of the Tamil community in the North of Sri Lanka, we are constrained to bring to your kind attention some important facts about our situation which the world should know.

The Sri Lankan government, while launching a massive military offensive against the Tamil people, has also imposed a tight censorship of the media and has barred all journalists - local and foreign - for the last six months - from coming to Jaffna. As a result there is no possibility of those outside the North knowing the whole truth about the war as well as the situation of the people here.

As a result of a series of army operations code-named 'Leap

Forward', 'Shake Hands' and 'Lightening Thunder' during the last few months, there was large-scale destruction of life, property, houses and institutions. Even Hindu temples, Christian churches and government schools which were thought safe by the refugees who flocked in were subject to aerial bombs and artillery shells. The death of over 120 refugees killed by six bombs within the precincts of the Navaly St. Peter's church and of twenty six young students in school uniform killed by an aerial bomb at Nager Kovil are worth mentioning here.

The above offensives have resulted already in waves of displacements towards the Jaffna town. And by the latest Army offensive, code-named 'Riviresa', about 500,000 people have been displaced and are living under inhuman conditions in the Thenmaratchy and Vadamaratchy areas of the Jaffna peninsula and also in the area South of Elephant Pass (Wanni district).

The government keeps reporting widely that adequate food supplies and medicines are being sent to the North. We wish to state that this is far from the truth. There is a dire shortage of food and medicines and the imminent danger of mass starvation and the spread of diseases.

The government insists on being the sole agent for channelling aid from international agencies thus denying our people even help from those sources. A few days ago three French doctors from the French Medicines Sans Frontier (MSF) were refused permission to come to Jaffna to help the woefully understaffed hospitals in our area.

There is also the urgent need of shelter and sanitary facilities to protect the half a million displaced people against the monsoonal rains and the spread of disease. It is required immediately and we need not remind the world that help delayed is help denied.

We would also like to draw your attention to the broader issues relating to the war. It has been proclaimed by the government that the

LTTE was totally responsible for the break-down of talks. It was well known that even the few decisions agreed on the first two rounds of talks were not implemented and there was an imminent danger of a breakdown of the talks. The LTTE for its part has already notified the government three weeks ahead of the danger of breakdown of the cessation of hostilities for lack of implementation. But the government was buying time for its political gains and did not consider the LTTE ultimatum as a serious warning prior to the breakdown of talks.

One of the reasons for the large exodus of people from the areas of conflict is the indiscriminate shelling and bombing carried out by the government forces. The war is proclaimed by the government as a war for peace and a war to liberate the people from the clutches of the LTTE. But in actual fact, it is a war of destruction for the people and their belongings. They flee the approaching army with fear and panic as if all hell was let loose before them.

We would appeal to you and other world leaders to exert maximum influence to bring an immediate halt to hostilities and enable the displaced people to return to their homes, and recommence their lives, however difficult it may be. This we trust can lead to steps towards a negotiated settlement and bring freedom, justice and peace for which all nationalities in Sri Lanka have craved.

Yours sincerely,

1. Nallai Gnanasambandar Adheenam, Nallur Temple, Jaffna.
2. Hindu Religious priest Organisation of North-East provinces.
3. Rev. Dr. S. Jebanesan, Bishop in Jaffna, Church of South India.
4. Miss. Thangamma Appacutty, Sri Durga Devi Devasthanam, Tellipalai.
5. Rev. Dr. J. Ambalavanar, Bishop Emeritus, Church of South India, Jaffna.
6. Rev. Dr. S. J. Emmanuel, Vicar General, Catholic Church, Jaffna Diocese.

Appendix iii.

<u>**Northern Province Principals' Association**</u>

Temporary address:
Hindu College
Chavakachcheri,
Sri Lanka.
03 - 12 - 1995

<u>**An appeal by the Northern Province Principals' Association**</u>

We the undersigned members of the Northern Province Principals' Association wish to place the following matters before you for your kind consideration.

The Tamil people who live in the North and East of Sri Lanka are a nation with a distinctive culture and education of their own. The North and East are their traditional homelands and this is borne out by historians. It is this traditional homeland we designate 'Tamil Eelam'. The European colonial powers in Ceylon - The Portuguese, the Dutch and the British - accepted the fact that the Tamils had a traditional homeland of their own. Successive Sinhala chauvinistic governments since Independence in 1948 adopted repressive policies against the Tamil people. Our representatives in parliament, in keeping with parliamentary democratic tradition, voiced demands for the Tamils' just rights and entered into pacts and agreements like the Bandaranaike-Chelvanayagam pact and the Dudley-Chelva agreement, but tragically, none of these pacts and agreements could be implemented due to the brute and unreasoning opposition of Sinhala-Buddhist chauvinist forces.

Further, there were ethnic riots in 1956, 1958, 1977, 1981 and 1983 which led to thousands of Tamils being killed and the looting of several millions worth of Tamils' property.

Our Tamil leaders banded together in 1974, adopted a resolution calling for the establishment of an independent state of Tamil Eelam which was endorsed by the Tamil people in the general election of 1977. But the oppression against the Tamils intensified. Continuing military repression decimated our nation even as Sinhala Buddhist chauvinism grabbed our traditional lands and destroyed our culture. At this juncture it became a historic imperative to resort to armed struggle to safeguard our rights. The Tamil Nation has accepted armed struggle as the only way out, the only salvation for the Tamils, the Liberation Tigers of Tamil Eelam (LTTE) emerged as the guardians of the Tamil people, firm in their convictions, fired by patriotism and steeled to sacrifice their lives for the cause they held sacred. Today it is only the LTTE which has captured the imagination and the hearts of the Tamil people. At this stage to try to separate the Tigers from the Tamil people is to be blind to a historical fact.

At a time when the Tamil Nation's right to self determination has been accepted internationally, the Sri Lankan government has climaxed its oppression of the Tamil people by launching a massive onslaught against them. The various military operations code named 'Leap Forward', 'Dragon Fire', 'Handshake' and 'Sunshine' have uprooted our people and destroyed our culture. Several hundreds of thousands of people resident in the Jaffna peninsula have been forced to flee their homes as a result of artillery shelling, aerial bombardment and the cannonade of tanks and gun boats.

These operations have resulted in the planned destruction of the education of our students.

We list below some of the discriminatory measures taken from time to time by the Sri Lankan state in the educational sphere.

1. The systematic destruction through standardisation of the higher education of Tamil students.

2. Impairing primary and secondary education through the gradual closing down of the five teachers' training colleges that were functioning in Jaffna.
3. The torching and bombing of libraries and schools.
4. Converting several schools into camps, both refugee and army.
5. Discrimination in the allocation of educational resources, thereby impeding the development of Tamil schools, in the following manner:

a. Non-supply of modern teaching aids.
b. Non-supply of laboratory and technical equipment.
c. Non-supply of chemicals
d. Failure to appoint teachers according to the school's needs.
e. Failure to provide adequate finance for new buildings and the purchase of furniture.
f. The embargo of fuel and electricity has made it impossible to use audio-visual aids to education.
g. Making it virtually impossible for our students to gain access to new publications and education-related information

6. Creating a situation whereby it becomes impossible for our students to pursue their studies. The climax of this process is the displacement of both teachers and students as a result of military operations.
7. The planned killing of students and teachers by the Sri Lankan state. As examples we cite the following:

a. Several students were severely injured during the aerial bombardment of Vadamaratchi.
b. Several teachers and students were killed when a Sri Lankan Pucara aircraft bombed St. Peter's Church, Navaly, during 'Operation Leap Forward'.

c. Over 25 students were killed and over 20 maimed for life when the Nagar Kovil Mahavidyalayam [college] was cluster-bombed.

d. Several students and teachers are among those killed during 'Operation Sunshine' when not only Valigamam but also Thenmaratchi and Vadamaratchi were simultaneously subjected to aerial bombardment, artillery shelling and gun-boat firing.

e. There were 454 schools catering to a large student population of 160, 218 (among these were several hundreds of displaced students from the Eastern province and the islands) in the Jaffna district. 106, 206 students and 3062 teachers from these schools are unable to continue their education as a result of this displacement. No civilised community or democratic society can condone a situation where a government wages war against a people saying it is for the liberation of the people, as the Sri Lankan government does against the Tamil people.

We urge that the following steps be taken to stop the military operations, which are the prime cause for the present predicament of the Tamil people, and enable a return to normalcy:

1. Accept the Eelam Tamils' right to self-determination.
2. Remove the Sinhala armed forces' camps in the Northern and Eastern provinces so that the people can live with security.
3. Attempt to negotiate a political solution with the Liberation Tigers who are the guardians of the Tamils and the spearhead of their freedom struggle.

We earnestly request the international educational community to co-operate with other forces to help ensure that the measures we have specified above are taken.

Thanking you

Yours sincerely,

Name

1. Mr. K. Shanmuganathapillai,
   Principal, Jaffna Central College
   Jaffna.

2 Mr. S. Kalatharan,
   Principal,
   Sir Waithilingam Thuraiswamy .M.V.
   Velani.

3. Mr. N. Anantharaj,
   Principal,
   Udupiddy American Mission College,
   Jaffna

4. Mr. K. Kanagasingam,
   Principal, Peripulam M.V,
   Valvettiturai,

5. Mr. V. Sivarasa,
   Principal, Kondavil Ramakrishna M.V,
   Jaffna.

6. Mr. P. Kamalanathan,
   Principal, Union College,
   Tellipallai.

7. Mr. K. Sandrasegara,
   Principal, Hindu College,
   Chavakachcheri.

8. Mr. A. M. Arunasalam,
   Principal,
   Manipay Memorial College,
   Manipay.

9. Mr. S. Nadarajah,
   Hartley College,
   Point Pedro.

10. Mr. A. Rajagopal,
    Principal, Senguntha Hindu College,
    Jaffna.

11. Mrs. L. Jayaveerasingam,
    Principal,
    Chundikuli Girls' College,
    Jaffna.

12. Mr. A. Panchalingam
    Principal,
    Jaffna Hindu College,
    Jaffna.

13. Mr. K. Thanapalasingam,
    Nadeswara College,
    Kankeshanthurai.

14. Mr. S. Balasubramaniam,
    Urumpirai Hindu College,
    Urumpirai.

15. Mr. T. Santhosam,
    J/ Vaidyeswara College,
    Jaffna.

16. Mrs. S. Jayarajah,
    Principal,
    J/ Hindu Ladies College,
    Jaffna.

17. Mrs. P. S. Skantharajah,
    Principal,
    J/ Vembadi Girls' High School,
    Jaffna.

18. Mr. V. Nimalanathan,
    Principal,
    J/Karampan Shanmugana M.V
    Kayts.

19. Mr. M. Kuddithamby,
    Principal,
    J/ Thevaraiyali Hindu College,
    Karaveddy.

20. Fr. J. B. Gnanapragasam,
    Principal,
    J/ St. Henry's College,
    Ilavalai.

21. Mrs. T. Balasingam,
    Principal,
    J/ Dr. A. Thiagarajah M. M. V,
    Karainakar.

22. Miss. K. Veerasingam,
    Principal,
    J/ Mahalir Maha Vidyalayam,
    Chavakachcheri.

Confederation of People's Organisations
Jaffna District
Temporarily: Dutch Road, Chavakachcheri, Sri Lanka

His Excellency Mr. Bill Clinton,   291 Stanley Road
The Right Honourable President of The U S A.,   Jaffna
The White House,
Washington.

23 November 1995

Esteemed Sir,

THE MEANINGLESS WAR WAGED BY THE SRI LANKAN
GOVERNMENT ON THE TAMIL PEOPLE

We the people's union of the Jaffna district, an organisation of more than a hundred general bodies of the district of Jaffna reflecting the ambitions and aspirations of the Tamil people send an urgent and essential message to the United States of America which attaches the paramount importance to democracy and individual freedom in international politics and to your excellency who assumed the leadership of it, for your excellency's consideration.

Your excellency is cognisant of the fact what we - Tamils - a national race of Sri Lanka, have been fighting for our political rights for a long time. At present we have fled Jaffna and sought shelter under the trees and along the roadsides in the areas of Vadamarachchi, Thenmarachchi and Vanni unable to face the brunt of ferocious atrocities and the onslaught, destruction and the unchecked atrocities of the Sri Lankan security forces bent on genocide. Thus half a million people have become refugees and they are under utter distress.

At this juncture the mass media owned and controlled by the Sri Lankan government carry on a propaganda based upon a press release purported to have been issued by an official of the South Asian affairs of your Ministry of Foreign Affairs. This news item being devoid of truth., spells out deep shock and anguish to the Tamils who are now forlorn and homeless. The alleged news item reads as follows: the cease-fire was broken by the LTTE and obstinacy and the propagation of violence of the LTTE caused the suffering of the people.

The president Chandrika Kumarathunga who got the mandate of the people by promising to start a dialogue with the LTTE to settle the problem of Tamils has broken it, and intensified the ethnic war.

The cessation of hostilities existed between the government of Sri Lanka and LTTE for about three months; during this period the government of Chandrika did not take any action to settle the ethnic problem. On the contrary, her government prepared for war and her activity created suspicion about her bonafides in the minds of Tamils.

The Actions taken by the Sri Lankan government during the cessation of hostilities

During the cessation of hostilities there were about two hundred violations by the Sri Lankan security forces. The government conducted a recruitment drive and allocated two thousand and five hundred million rupees in the budget for the needs of war. The government did not make any sincere effort in settling the ethnic problem through political dialogue. The government refused to make the cessation of hostilities a permanent cease-fire and to fulfill the basic political ambitions of the Tamil people.

Due to these factors the LTTE became suspicious of the government of Sri Lanka. It assumed that the government of Sri Lanka was trying to strengthen itself militarily to crush the political ambitions of the

112

Tamil people by drawing out of the political talks. So understanding the subtle intentions of the government of Chandrika the LTTE set a dead line to the talks and demanded an immediate solution to some important problems of the Tamil people.

They demanded the lifting of the economic blockade and the transport blockade. But the government of Sri Lanka failed to act positively. Because of this negative approach of the government an unfortunate situation of breaking the cessation of hostilities arose.

Without trying to solve the political problems of the Tamil people the government of Chandrika bought time in preparing for a military solution.

Thus we claim that irresponsibility of the government of Chandrika inevitably led to the breaking of the cessation of hostilities.

Now the cause of all the sufferings of the Tamil people is the army occupation and the irresponsible attitude of the government. The Sri Lankan army has occupied most parts of the North and East. Since the beginning of the ethnic war fifty thousand people have been killed. Millions and millions of rupees worth of properties have been destroyed. Throughout the country fifteen lakhs of Tamil people have become refugees. They lead a sorrowful life deprived of the basic human rights.

It is proved that the Sri Lankan army has been indulging in many terrorist activities in the North and East. It generated violence which resulted in genocide. The government has been implementing the economic blockade since 1990. The Sri Lankan government and its army continue to oppress the Tamil people. We wish to point out that it is not acceptable to put the blame on the LTTE for our sufferings.

We wish to remind your excellency that many international human rights organisations have vehemently condemned the Sri Lankan army's atrocities. Yet the Sri Lankan government has not taken any constructive action. On the 18th of February 1995, we conducted a procession, in which, many lakhs of people took part in Jaffna and appealed to the president of Sri Lanka to solve the ethnic problem in a peaceful manner. But she failed to respond.

Reposing absolute confidence in the goodwill and bonafides of your excellency, at this critical juncture we respectfully request your honour to take such steps as your honour deems to redress the adverse repercussions arising out of a statement reportedly made by an official of your government which not only honour democracy and human rights but also recognises the importance and impact of the minorities' just struggle against the oppressors for their survival.

Thank you Sir,

Yours sincerely

President   Secretary
(Solomon S. Cyril)   (P. Kanagalingam)

Appendix v.

JAFFNA CITIZENS' COMMITTEE
(Temporarily: Holy Family Convent, Mirusuvil, Thenmaratchi, Sri Lanka)
115, Fourth cross Street, Jaffna

Patrons:
Rt. Rev. Dr. T. Saundranayagam
Bishop of Jaffna

Thangammah Appakkuddy
Trustee,
Thurgai Amman Temple
Tellipalai

S. Paramadhdhariya Swamigal
Chief, Nallai Atheenam

President:
Professor K. Kunaratnam
Vice - Chancellor,
University of Jaffna

Vice President:
S. Selvendra B sc. F. C. A.
Chartered Accountant

Secretary:
R. Mahendran
Principal.
J/ Kokuvil Hindu College.

Mr. Boutros Boutros Gali,
Secretary General,
UNO

27 . 11. 1995

Dear Sir,

The ethnic conflict in Sri Lanka and The Tamil National problem

We invite your kind attention to our letter dated 5th October 1995, appealing to you to exert pressure on the Sri Lankan president Hon. Mrs. Chandrika Bandaranaike Kumaranatunga to stop the military oppression against the Tamils in this island and to initiate steps to resolve the ethnic conflict in Sri Lanka through negotiations. In that

115

letter we warned that the continued military operation will have disastrous effects on the civilians. We are constrained to bring to your notice that the Sri Lankan army advance on Jaffna, the heartland of the Tamils, has resulted in the exodus of around half a million people from their homes in the Jaffna region.

The launching of the latest military operation in a densely populated region such as Valigamam and the heartless manner in which bombs and shells are fired indiscriminately into built up areas located even far away from the theatre of war has resulted in the deaths of many men, women and children and injuries to many others. In addition, colossal damage has been done to civilian and government properties in the region.

These military operations coming on top of the numerous oppressive measures against the Tamils that are already in force for quite some time, shows that the Sri Lankan government is not concerned about the safety, security or the well-being of the Tamil people or their political and human rights. It is only preoccupied with the use of the military to keep in a most contemptuous and callous manner, the unwilling Tamils under its illegitimate control. At a time when there is increasing recognition by member states of the UNO, of the National and human rights of the Tamil people, Sri Lankan government is violating those rights blatantly. The safety and security of the Tamils are not guaranteed in any part of Sri Lanka now. Can the International community be a silent spectator to the alarming turn of events in this island and continue to tolerate the abuse of state power by the Sri Lankan government against the Tamil people? We feel that it is incumbent upon the world body to take the initiative to dissuade the Sri Lankan government from pursuing its military aggression and to sponsor a political solution to the Tamil National problem in this island. The need for initiating such a course of action can be seen from the following facts in addition to several others.

1. Historically the Tamil people and the Sinhalese people in this island have been two distinctly separate peoples, each constituting a separate Nation.

2. The two peoples were brought together under a single Sri Lankan polity by the departing British colonial administrators. Successive Sri Lankan governments have attempted to militarily keep the Tamils under subjugation denying their rights including their inalienable right for self-determination.

3. A closer look at the historical facts since 1931 will reveal that the Sinhalese political leaders in collaboration with some British administrative officials enacted a constitution in 1948 which denied the political and other rights of the Tamil people and helped the Sinhalese to consolidate their political power. Neither this constitution nor the subsequent constitutions enacted by the Sinhala majority governments received the mandate of the Tamil people and thus these constitutions have no legitimacy over the Tamils.

4. The present military advance, displacing lakhs of Tamils from their homes is in effect an invasion of the Tamil homeland by the Sinhalese security forces. The government, if it considers the Tamils as part of the Sri Lankan Nation, will not use heavy weapons in built up civilian areas causing death and destruction on a large scale and impose an embargo on the transport of food and other essential items to the Tamils in the North and East.

5. Tamils have agitated by peaceful means for several decades to win their rights and the attempts by successive governments to militarily suppress them have not diminished their determination to continue their struggle to attain their goal.

We appeal to you to bring to the notice of the member states the fast deteriorating situation in this island and initiate steps to compel the

117

Sri Lankan government to withdraw its armed forces from the Tamil homeland so that the Tamil people can get back to their homes and live in peace. We request you to take all necessary steps to bring about a negotiated political settlement which satisfies the political aspirations of the Tamil people which have been suppressed by the armed might of successive Sri Lankan governments since independence.

We also appeal to you to request the member states of the UNO to take urgent steps to provide financial and material assistance for food, shelter and sanitation direct through the NGOs to alleviate the suffering of nearly half a million Tamil people who have been displaced and rendered destitute overnight by the callous military operation of the Sri Lankan security forces.

Yours sincerely,

K. Kunaratnam   R. Mahendran
President   Secretary
JAFFNA CITIZEN'S COMMITTEE

University of Jaffna, Sri Lanka
Thirunelvely, Jaffna, Sri Lanka

Secretary to The Ministry
of Foreign Affairs
of The United States of America
Washington D.C
U. S. A

Temporary Address:
Hindu College,
Chavakachcheri,
Sri Lanka.

21st. November 1995

Dear Sir,

      During the second week of this month the Sri Lankan Broadcasting Corporation repeatedly broadcast the following statement as made by an official of the South Asian Bureau of The Foreign Affairs of the U. S. A.

'The adamant attitude of the LTTE in pursuing violence is the main cause for the sufferings of the Tamils. The cessation of hostilities was broken entirely by the LTTE'.

We were shocked and saddened by the above reported statement beamed repeatedly by the government media. We the community of the University of Jaffna wish to place before you the following facts contradicting the above statement.

1. The LTTE has emerged as the only organised and accepted leadership that is leading the Tamils against all forms of oppressions inflicted on the Tamils by the Sinhala governments. We cannot subscribe to the government's mere wishful thinking that Tamils and LTTE are entirely two separate entities and that the people want to be liberated from the LTTE.

119

For a long time the Tamil community has been deliberately deceived by successive Sinhala politicians and their governments. For more than thirty years (1949 - 1983) at every denial of the rights of the Tamils, the latter have expressed their opposition by parliamentary, democratic and non-violent forms. But these oppositions were put down by inhuman militaristic forces of the state. It is the arrogant refusal to respond to democratic oppositions and the militaristic excesses committed by the state forces that pushed the Tamil youths to resort to militancy in order to protect the Tamils and defend their rights.

2. The reported statement of the American official that the cessation of hostilities was broken entirely by the LTTE is far from the truth. During the cessation of hostilities talks were held between the government and the LTTE. But what happened at the talks and how seriously they were conducted by the government is crucial to understand why it was given up by the LTTE.

Even the decisions arrived at during the first round of talks were not implemented. The government trumpeted to the world over that the economic embargo against the Tamil regions was to a great extent lifted. But the truth was that even after a week of these announcements the military officers at the check points at Vavuniya did not allow the people to carry the items which were announced by the government stating that they have not received the gazette notification. But the same military officers were quick in receiving the clamp down of the embargo within hours of the breaking of cessation of hostilities. We consider this action of the military a good example for the usual conduct of the government with regard to implementation of government decisions.

3. We like to point out the LTTE, already a month before the actual date (19th of April 1995), had informed the government of the non-implementation of decisions reached and also given other reasons for

a possible break down in the cessation of hostilities. But the government disregarded these warnings and dragged on four months without any meaningful talks or implementation of decisions in order to gain political and military advantage. They did not show any urgency in relieving the sufferings of the Tamil people by allowing the basic requirements of life.

4. When Mrs. Chandrika Bandaranaike Kumaratunga was elected president, it was the LTTE who first gave the good will signs towards a possible cease-fire. They unconditionally released prisoners of war, called for a permanent cease-fire, publicly announced a symbolic cease-fire and observed it unilaterally for over a week, welcomed the independent and peace loving NGO representatives from the south and expressed their wish for a permanent cease-fire.

The government did not pay serious attention to the above good will moves. Finally when they agreed for a cessation of hostilities (not a cease-fire as wished by the LTTE) and started talks, the LTTE had repeatedly requested that the government to send true representatives who were empowered to take political decisions. But the government kept on sending persons who were mere architects and bankers without any political background or ability. Such acts clearly demonstrated the government was not taking the talks seriously enough.

It is impossible that your esteemed country which concerns itself well with the politics of the whole world and having the resources to engage in such work failed to know the facts around the breaking of the cessation of hostilities. How come that the statement of an official of your ministry contradicts these facts?

Because of the high esteem the Tamils have of your country, the reported statement coming over the government's media has hurt the feeling of our people who are already suffering immense hardships.

Your country which stands up and protects democratic and human rights all over the world, we believe, will not approve or encourage the actions of the S.L. government with respect to human right violations. But the above statement appears to encourage the anti-human right actions of the present government.

Although we doubt the authenticity of the above statement, it has hurt the feelings of our suffering people. Hence we hope that the people and government of USA will take all remedial measures as early as possible to restore justice and peace in this country.

Thank you,

Yours sincerely,

For the university of Jaffna

1. Dr. C. S. Natchinakiniar	Head / Dept. of Community medicine
2. Dr. K. Sivapalan	Head / Dept. of Physiology
3. Mr. R. Nandakumaran	Senior lecturer / Dept. of economics
4. Miss. S. Arulanantham	Assist. Librarian
5. Prof. A. Sanmugathas	Head / Dept. Tamil and music
6. Mr. R. Jegatheesan	Senior Assist. Internal Auditor
7. Mr. R. Rajeswaran	Assist. registrar / Dept. of library service
8. Mr. S. Thevethasan	Staff Officer (Statistics)
9. Mr. A. Antonyrajan	Lecturer

Copies to:
1. Director, South Asian Bureau of the Foreign Affairs
2. Ambassador for USA in Sri Lanka.
3. Speaker, Congress of America.

4. High Commissioner for UNHCR.
5. Chairman, The Senate.
6. Resident representative ICRC.
7. The press.

Appendix vii.

The translated version of the message sent by Mr. V. Pirabakaran, Leader of the LTTE to the people and leaders of Tamil Nadu

> LTTE Headquarters,
> Tamil Eelam,
> 28. 12. 95

On behalf of our people, I wish to express my affection and gratitude to the people and leaders of Tamil Nadu for voicing passionately for the Tamils of Eelam who are struggling for their liberation against the genocidal oppression of the Sinhala regime.

The waves of sympathy that sweeps across Tamil Nadu whenever the Eelam Tamils are repressed has always been a deterrent to our ruthless enemy and a great source of hope and relief to our aggrieved people. It also impresses upon the world that the Eelam Tamils are not alone without support. Even though several forces have been making deliberate efforts to pollute the minds of the Tamils of Tamil Nadu with ill-conceived notions about our national struggle and about the Liberation Tigers who lead that struggle, we are encouraged and emboldened to note that there is growing upsurgence in Tamil Nadu demanding justice for our people on the basis of ethnic affinity and humanism.

For a long time even before the birth of the LTTE, the Tamil Nation has been bleeding. For a long time, our nation has been facing genocide. In this lengthy history, extending over four decades, our language, our culture, our education, our economic existence - all the essential elements that form the very basis of our national life - have been subjected to systematic destruction. The monster of Sinhala racism has been usurping our motherland. The Sinhala armed forces have occupied our historical cities and towns. Hundreds of thousands of people have been forced to vacate their own lands and reduced to destitution. In this tragic history tainted with blood, forty thousand Tamils have been exterminated. The current war is a continuation and monstrous expansion of this cruel genocidal history.

Historically the Eelam Tamils are faced with blatant genocide. This well-planned racial extermination is aimed at the destruction of the national identity of the Tamils. Its true face is masked by false propaganda. We regret that the international community has not yet understood this phenomenon.

The political struggle of the people of Tamil Eelam has been pitted against the Sinhala racist oppression which is aimed at the genocidal destruction of the Tamil Nation. For more than quarter of a century our past generation fought non-violent struggles based on the principles of Ahimsa enunciated by Mahatma Gandhi. But the Sinhala racist state did not understand or appreciate the spiritual and moral values of non-violent struggles. Ahimsa agitations were brutally crushed by armed violence. With the repression of democratic non-violent struggles racial extermination assumed a dangerous proportion. It was when the Tamil people had no choice other than to take arms to defend themselves, the Tamil Tiger movement and the armed struggle gave birth.

The Sinhala state has been making desperate efforts to characterise the mode of armed resistance based on the struggle of self-determination as a form of 'terrorism' and 'separatism'. These ill-conceived notions are being propagated among the Indian people and among the international community. This malicious propaganda is aimed at distorting the truth and discrediting the mode of our struggle. We are neither terrorists nor separatists, nor propagators of 'armed culture'. We are fighting for a noble cause. We are fighting to protect our people from racial annihilation. We are compelled to take up arms against the armed violence which has taken a genocidal form. We are faced with a complex conflictual historical situation in which

125

we have to struggle with our lives for the right to live. We fervently hope that the people of Tamil Nadu and India will understand our critical situation.

The successive Sinhala-Buddhist racist governments, since Independence, have attempted to subjugate and dominate our people instead of integrating them. This has compelled our people to decide to determine their own political destiny. As a people constituting themselves with the structural elements of a national formation, they are entitled to the right to self-determination. It is only when state repression assumed the dangerous dimension of genocide our people chose to invoke their inherent right to self-determination. The mandate to fight for self-determination was given by our people to the old leadership, before the growth of the armed resistance movement. The political objective and the struggle of our movement is based on this political will of our people. It is those who lack a clear vision of the history and legitimacy of the struggle for self-determination in Tamil Eelam attempt to characterise us as 'separatists'. This attempt to portray the legitimate struggle of our people, who aspire to live as free beings with dignity and security liberated from the peril of national destruction, as 'separatism' and to compare and confuse it with the internal problems of the Indian states is misleading and wrong.

The hope and expectation of our people that the Sinhala nation might offer an alternative to the demand of an Independent state are now shattered. The Sinhala nation is not prepared to recognise the historically constituted traditional lands in which the Tamils lived for centuries as the homeland of the Tamils. It is for the resolution of this crucial issue that the Tamils have been cheated for a long time. Tamil political history is full of incidents of abrogation of pacts and agreements on this basic issue.

The Chandrika government has scored historical achievements in the task of destroying the geographical unity and integrity of the Tamil homeland and disrupting the national life of the Tamils. Having cheated the world with the slogans of 'War for Peace' and 'Liberating the Tamils', her regime has occupied our historical homeland. The central theme of her proposed package is aimed at re-defining the geographical structure of the Tamil homeland.

From the time of Bandaranaike to Chandrika's period, successive Sinhala racist states have adopted repressive military policies instead of a peaceful approach to resolve the conflict. Chandrika's approach is unique. Misguiding the world under the slogan of peace, she has ingeniously planned and executed a genocidal strategy against the Tamils.

Our Talks with Chandrika have ended in fiasco. The Chandrika regime refused to create conditions of peace and normalcy by relaxing military and economic pressure on the Tamils. Her government was reluctant to enter into a permanent cease-fire with international supervision. Instead, under the guise of a fragile cessation of hostilities, the government has been strengthening its military machine. It refused to open up a land route to the people by relaxing the siege of Jaffna. It gave primacy to the hegemonic interests of the military rather than to create an environment of peace.

The government did not give any importance to the peace talks with the LTTE. It delegated ordinary bureaucrats to the peace negotiations. High-ranking political leaders did not participate. The government did not reveal its package of proposals during the peace talks with the LTTE.

The Chandrika government failed to take seriously our proposition that we were prepared to consider a political framework that recognises the Tamil homeland with full form of autonomy to the Tamils. We expressed our goodwill by releasing prisoners of war. Yet, the Chandrika government was not prepared even to settle the minor day to day problems of our people. We felt that the government was not sincerely interested in resolving the ethnic conflict by negotiating with the LTTE. We were also convinced that the Chandrika regime was not prepared to offer any substantial political framework that would satisfy the political aspirations of the Tamils. Under these circumstances, when the talks prolonged meaninglessly we issued deadlines. But the government did not take our warnings seriously. The talks collapsed. Having created conditions for the breakdown of talks the government blamed the LTTE. It carried out a false propaganda campaign internationally that the LTTE was against the peace approach. In truth, it was Chandrika's government which was opposed to peace.

Claiming that the Tamil people are the citizens of the country, Chandrika's regime has embarked on a massive military onslaught on the Tamils. Having assembled a formidable force in a single battle front it has occupied the historic city of Jaffna and has raised the Sinhalese national flag over our soil. The Sinhala nation is celebrating this tragic event soaked by the tears of five hundred thousand displaced Tamils. Celebrations are taking place in Colombo as if the Tamil nation was defeated at war. We do not believe that the Sinhalese chauvinists who have deeply hurt the national sentiments of the Tamils in such a manner would offer justice to the Tamils.

The Tamil nation which has been conducting a heroic freedom struggle for such a long time, will not be frustrated by a setback in a single battle. Our people are fiercely determined though they have faced the enormous suffering arising from death, destruction, displacement and destitution. We are united and determined by the passion for freedom. We are confident that the setbacks of today will turn out to be the victories of tomorrow. We are firmly convinced that our land which bleeds today will become a free land one day.

Though our enemy has been adopting devious methods to alienate us from the outside world, from the world Tamil community and from Tamil Nadu where our deep roots are embedded, the support and sympathy generating from Tamil Nadu have given us moral inspiration and determination.

128

We are deeply saddened to note a recent incident in Trichi where a youth has taken his life by self-immolation as an extreme form of expression of solidarity. While we pay our respects to his passion for freedom and his sentiments of ethnic love we feel that such acts of self-sacrifice are unnecessary and therefore have to be avoided.

The Sinhala racist state is firmly determined to continue to carry out the genocidal war in Tamil Eelam. In these circumstances, Tamil Nadu should continue to voice for our plight and express support to our legitimate cause. This is what the people of Tamil Eelam fervently expect from the people of Tamil Nadu.

Yours sincerely,
(V. Pirabakaran)
Leader
Liberation Tigers of Tamil Eelam